λ

$\mathcal{A}$ Word Before . . .

"*There now. . . .*"

I can hear her say it in my heart.

"A hot cup of tea, maybe a warm bath, two aspirin, and you will feel better soon."

My mama had such a simple answer for stress. Because of her faith in the formula, my four sisters and I were easily convinced — and it seemed to work. Especially the cup of tea part.

She often shared it with us, and we got the chance to "visit it out."

Why not try it? As I visit with you from the memory bank of the Word of God, and my own life . . .

Pour yourself a cup of tea, take a few minutes out to
relax
renew
remember and
rejoice!

With the help of Lou Ann Smith, I have written these thoughts down with the prayer that God will use them to remind you of His numberless benefits, accrued to your account.

As you read, why not have a pad of sticky notes nearby and write some memos to yourself?

- Ask God to hang some words from the Word in the Museum of your Memory
- Consider ways you can create some memorials for those coming after you.

Remember with me what Peter wrote:

> "I . . . keep on reminding you of these things, even though you already know them. . . ."

"A lift for people who need to be refreshed."
BARBARA JOHNSON
Author of
STICK A GERANIUM IN YOUR HAT AND BE HAPPY

Forget Not His Blessings

CELEBRATING
WHAT GOD
HAS DONE
FOR YOU

DAISY HEPBURN
with Lou Ann Smith

THOMAS NELSON PUBLISHERS
NASHVILLE

Published in Nashville, Tennessee, by Thomas Nelson, Inc.

Unless otherwise noted, Scripture quotations are from the NEW KING JAMES VERSION of the Bible. Copyright ©   1979, 1980, 1982, Thomas Nelson, Inc., Publishers.

Scripture quotations noted TLB are from The Living Bible (Wheaton, Illinois: Tyndale House Publishers, 1971) and are used by permission.

Scripture quotations noted THE AMPLIFIED BIBLE are from THE AMPLIFIED BIBLE: Old Testament. Copyright © 1962, 1964 by Zondervan Publishing House (used by permission); and from THE AMPLIFIED NEW TESTAMENT. Copyright © 1958 by the Lockman Foundation (used by permission).

Scripture quotations noted NIV are from The Holy Bible: NEW INTERNATIONAL VERSION. Copyright © 1978 by the New York International Bible Society. Used by permission of Zondervan Bible Publishers.

Scripture quotations noted J.B. PHILLIPS are from J.B. PHILLIPS: THE NEW TESTAMENT IN MODERN ENGLISH, Revised Edition. Copyright © J.B. Phillips 1958, 1960, 1972. Used by permission of Macmillan Publishing Co., Inc.

Scripture quotations noted RSV are from the REVISED STANDARD VERSION of the Bible. Copyright © 1946, 1952, 1971, 1973 by the Division of Christian Education of the National Council of the Churches of Christ in the U.S.A. Used by permission.

Printed in the United States of America

1 2 3 4 5 6 7 - 98 97 96 95 94 93

To Emily,

whose precious new life
reminded me to write this down
before I forget . . .

Acknowledgments

*B*efore I forget—

Let me acknowledge with deep gratitude God's continuing work in my life. He has provided opportunities for me to travel thousands of miles each year. The people I have met, who have ministered to me even as I speak to them, have encouraged me to write down the collage of thoughts and memories in this book.

In these pages you will find glimpses of family members who have contributed to my life and therefore to the message of this book.

Although it is dedicated to our first grandchild, Emily Elizabeth Magnuson, it is also offered as a tribute to friends, Prayer Partners, and to the many who have encouraged my life and shared their walks with Jesus with me.

To Lou Ann Smith, who patiently, skillfully, interpreted through her heart and computer my words on tapes, I owe a continuing debt of love and gratitude.

Is there a way to acknowledge the support and loyalty of a husband with whom I have shared over forty years? Perhaps not fully, but with all my heart! What memories!

"I thank my God upon every remembrance of you."
Please don't forget that!

Daisy

Contents

Part One

— ❀ —

*W*hat
Benefits
to
Remember!

Chapter 1

*B*efore I Forget . . .

Bless the Lord, O my soul,
And forget not all His benefits.
(Ps. 103:2)

"*M*y goodness — what an unusual gift!"

Please don't tell my sister I said that. But that was my first reaction.

The small package arrived early in November. But when I read *Do not open until Christmas* in bold print I recognized once again that Ruth was ahead of the game in holiday preparations. The box was lightweight. I shook it gently and listened for a clue.

Now, those who know me well, including Ruth, understand that I am unable to resist the urge to open a personal gift, card, postal delivery, or even a can of soup. She had to be kidding. Besides, I reasoned for about a second before tearing off the brown paper, how would she know? We are separated by nearly three thousand miles.

Memorial Pearls

It only took an instant to get the packaging materials out of the way. Then I stared at the interesting object. I was glad I was alone. It wasn't exactly what I expected. But that was before I understood its profound significance.

It looked like a miniature, homemade hat box. Something a youngster might craft for a school project and bestow upon Mom for Mother's Day.

How would you react?

About four inches in diameter and two inches deep, it had purple felt and silver glitter glued on the top. Edging the circumference of the lid was a string of pearls. Right in the middle Ruth had tenderly fastened an old brooch with more pearls arranged like a sunburst in an imitation gold setting.

Because it didn't seem to weigh much more than a few feathers, it didn't occur to me that there might be another gift inside the keepsake box. But I opened it anyway and there, resting on the purple felt lining was a simple, three-by-five card, folded in half. My eyes stung with happy tears as I read its message:

> Daisy,
> This little token of our love was made
>   with tender care.
> I took apart some jewelry that Mama used
>   to wear
> and fastened pieces to the top — to decorate
>   with glue,
> Each bead and pin I hope will have some
>   meaning just for you!
> Ruth and Gordon

She signed their names in red and green ink and drew holly

leaves and Christmas bells around the words. I looked again at the memory box. I hadn't even recognized those pieces of jewelry. But now I smiled even while my eyes continued to cloud up at the thought of our precious mama, who is now in heaven, and how she enjoyed occasionally wearing a piece of inexpensive costume jewelry to look fancy — especially for Daddy.

Raised in a conservative Christian home, Mama was taught that beauty shouldn't come from outward adornment. To a humble woman such as she, wearing beads and earrings, which were often hand-me-downs, was an extravagance that tickled her like it would a young girl playing dress-up.

I sat down on the couch and ran my fingers around the string of forty-eight faux pearls. And as I did, those small, smooth gems became, for me, touchstones — linking me to memories of a godly woman who lived her simple life in a way that witnessed God's glory.

And, though I'm certain Mama's pearls weren't exactly what Bible prophets like Joshua had in mind, I remembered that the Word of God clearly teaches the importance of building into our lives "memorial stones" that serve to keep fresh in our hearts the solid truth of Scripture.

Old Testament Pearls

The fourth chapter of the Old Testament book of Joshua gives account of the importance God places on memorial stones. After the Israelites' incredible journey through the wilderness, they were finally within reach of the Promised Land. There, at the Jordan river, the Lord performed a miracle. He dried up that raging torrent so His people could cross on dry land.

I can imagine that every person was anxious to move on. But just when they were about to proceed, Joshua stopped them. God had instructed him to do something that, I'm sure, struck his listeners as a most unusual exercise after all they'd been through in the wilderness and all the miracles of God they had witnessed. Maybe they questioned his judgment. Would not the next move have been to hurry in and claim that long-awaited land of milk and honey?

Instead, God told Joshua to listen for an urgent message. As soon as he received it, he passed it along to twelve chosen men, one from each tribe of Israel:

> Cross over before the ark of the LORD your God into the midst of the Jordan, and each one of you take up a stone on his shoulder, according to the number of the tribes of the children of Israel, that this may be a sign among you when your children ask in time to come, saying, "What do these stones mean to you?" Then you shall answer them that the waters of the Jordan were cut off before the ark of the covenant of the LORD; when it crossed over the Jordan, the waters of the Jordan were cut off. And these stones shall be for a memorial to the children of Israel forever.
>
> (Josh. 4:5-7)

Modern Gems

What a wonderful idea! Leaving a solid reminder of God's presence and protection would give hope to many generations to come. What a gem of a tradition for us to pick up on, don't you think? And I'm delighted to know there are still believers building monuments to the glory of God today.

After speaking at a women's retreat in the Midwest, I received a lovely photograph from a dear woman I met there named Priscilla. In her letter she wrote:

"I'm sending you a picture of my father, Carl Ahline, eighty-seven years old, from Galesburg, Illinois. He is standing by the hitching post that my husband's father, Myron Freeburg of Minneapolis, gave to us before he died. The stone came from our Grandfather Freeburg's farm in St. Cloud, Minnesota."

Priscilla's father is pictured resting his hand on a large marker stone. The stone has a clear inscription: *No greater joy can I have than this, to hear that my children follow the truth* (3 John 4 RSV).

What a beautiful, tangible, modern-day memorial stone. "This stone has inspired thoughts and comments from many people," Priscilla told me. "It gives us great strength."

No Greater Joy Than Remembering

Inspiration. Motivation. Encouragement. Strength to go on. That was the purpose of memorial stones in Old Testament times. It can be my purpose, too. And yours.

The psalmist wrote:

> Give ear, O my people, to my law;
> Incline your ears to the words of my mouth.
> I will open my mouth in a parable;
> I will utter dark sayings of old,
> Which we have heard and known,
> And our fathers have told us.
> We will not hide them from their children.
> Telling to the generation to come the praises of the
>   LORD,

And His strength and His wonderful works that He has
done.

For He established a testimony in Jacob,
And appointed a law in Israel,
Which He commanded our fathers,
That they should make them known to their children;
That the generation to come might know them,
The children who would be born,
That they may arise and declare them to their children,
That they may set their hope in God,
And not forget the works of God.

(Ps. 78:1-7)

Forget Not His Benefits

Forget not His glorious miracles. How often the Bible reminds
us of this. The memory is a wonderful tool. When triggered,
stored information can play in our minds like a videocassette
recording. When lessons of truth from history are handed down
from generation to generation our hope is set anew on God.

Even unpleasant memories serve to teach us valuable lessons
and bring us hope. Have you ever had a clumsy or unfortunate
experience, like a fender-bender or getting lost in a strange city,
and you said, "Someday we'll laugh about this"? That's what I
mean. Some events are etched in our memories, and we learn
about life from them.

Some happenings (no matter how much we'd like to) we never
forget. For instance, I'll never forget October 17, 1989.

Shaking Up My Memory

It had been a pretty average day. There was work to be done at Bridgemont, the high school in San Francisco that my husband presides over. We started at nine o'clock in the morning by convening a meeting of "The Little Red Hens," a women's auxiliary group at the school. After that I led a Bible study, returned phone calls, attended meetings, planned for upcoming travel, and tackled an endless to-do list. David's day was similarly hectic. Sound like one of yours?

Later that day, finally home, David and I were looking forward to an evening of cheering on the Oakland A's and the Giants, who were promising an exciting World Series.

"Get out the folding trays," I told David, who was already positioning the TV. "I'm going downstairs to take a bath [a personal form of stress management] and when I finish it'll just be an intimate evening of Lean Cuisine and you-n-me — and the fifty thousand people at Candlestick Park."

Sounds romantic, doesn't it?

I clicked on the answering machine, filled the tub with Calgon-take-me-away, and settled in for a mini-vacation when the unbelievable happened. A truly moving experience.

"Lord!" I prayed as waves in the tub crested and rolled, "You've got to be kidding!" I was thinking that I'm certainly not afraid to go to heaven — but I had no intention of going without my bathrobe!

Seismologists reported the earthquake that rocked Candlestick Park stadium, the famous Golden Gate Bridge, and the Hepburn basement bathtub measured 7.1 on the Richter scale.

Who Could Forget?

Who could ever forget the devastation delivered upon thousands of people as the Bay Bridge gave way and the Embarcadero freeway collapsed? Those images are burned forever in our thoughts.

Do you want to know what other image is uniquely burned in my memory banks from that experience? First, let me tell you I've given the best forty years of my life to David Hepburn. Not a minute—not even a second—of all that time do I regret. We've learned to be loyal to one another. Caring. Always watching out for each other.

So, when pictures started falling off the walls, our favorite porcelain tea set moved to a new location on its own, and I was sure I heard a train roaring through our living room, you can imagine what David did, can't you?

He did what probably any noble, sensitive man would do in the heat of a crisis. *He forgot me.* Yep! He ran right out the front door. He took off to save his skin while I was left sailing on stormy seas, rocking and rolling, and yelling at seventy-eight rpm: "David! Davidwhereareyou? David! Get me out of here! David! I can't stand up!"

Try to Remember

It only took a moment for my husband to remember to come back for me. Maybe you've had a dramatic experience or two. If so, you know that some life experiences are cemented in our memories. Try as we may, we'll never pry them loose. Others slip away.

Who knows why I remember fifteen old phone numbers from thirty years ago that are useless to me now but I can't remember what I went upstairs to get? I've started to make lists and write down important reminders . . . but sometimes I forget where I wrote them down!

There is one list written down for me already that I can always find. It's a special memo. "Bless the LORD, O my soul," the psalmist wrote, "and forget not all His benefits" (Ps. 103:2).

Why should we remember? Because God's benefits give us hope. They can be spiritual pearls to remind us of our heritage. Rejoice as you think about them.

God's Memo
(from Psalm 103)

O my soul, don't forget the Lord's benefits! He
- forgives all your iniquities
- heals all your diseases
- redeems your life from destruction (the grave)
- crowns you with lovingkindness and tender mercies
- satisfies your mouth with good things
- administers righteousness (justice) and judgment (fairness) to all who are oppressed
- revealed His ways to Moses, His acts (dealings) to the people of Israel
- is merciful and gracious
- is slow to anger (patiently considerate)
- is plenteous (abounding) in mercy

- will not always chide (show hostility) nor maintain His anger forever
- has not dealt with us to the measure of our sins nor regarded us as our iniquities deserve
- shows mercy toward those who fear (revere) Him — mercy as high as the heavens are above the earth
- has removed our transgressions from us as far as the east is from the west (symbol of infinity)
- tenderly sympathizes with those who revere Him as a father has compassion for his children (because He remembers what we are made of)
- displays His mercy (faithful love), which rests eternally upon those who fear (revere) Him
- causes His righteousness to rest on the children's children
- rules over all.

Bless the Lord, O my soul!

I'll Never Forget—But in Case I Do

I'm so thankful for the time my precious sister Ruth took to lovingly craft a memory keepsake box for me and for our other three sisters. How I love remembering Mama and the great God she served.

That simple box was a new beginning for me. Now I'm collecting memorial stones and placing them here and there in my life. Like precious pearls of wisdom, they will be cultivated and discussed and passed along to my children's children. When future generations of the Hepburn heritage ask, "What are these?" someone will answer, "They're memorial stones to

remind us: Forget not! God's tremendous blessings in our lives."
For there are many.

And, like a string of pearls laced throughout the years, they
will touch for us uplifting remembrances of our God, Jehovah.

Memo to myself:
   *Put a few stones around the house . . . perhaps
Emily will ask me what they are for—and I will tell
her!*

Prayer:
   *Dear Lord, I am so prone to forget all the daily mira-
cles You perform for me. Help me to recognize some
stones in what I thought were uncrossable rivers.
Amen.*

Before I forget—I'll do it today:
   *When have you received a gift you didn't appreci-
ate—until later?*
   What made it precious?
   *Has God ever given you a gift that appeared trite or
unpolished—but became beautiful?*
   *How can you begin to mark God's movement in your
life with some form of memorial stones?*

Part Two

—— ❁ ——

*W*hat
God
Remembers...
And
Forgets

Chapter 2

*D*one ... What?

[He] forgives all your iniquities. ...
(Ps. 103:3)

*D*id you ever forget something really important — something you desperately needed to remember?

"Of course!" you say. "Is that a trick question?"

How about this: Did you ever remember something you desperately wanted to forget? "Hmmmmm." That can be painful.

God has a wonderful ability toward our failures. Let me tell you a long-ago and far-away story that is precious to my own heart and illustrates what I mean.

Once Upon a Time

One hundred and thirteen years ago, in a small seaport in southern England, a little girl named Elizabeth was told by her mother to go and buy a fish for dinner. Though she was only twelve and small for her age, Elizabeth was strong and healthy and quite independent.

She always did as she was told and on this drizzly Sunday

afternoon, as the fog began to roll in from the ocean, Elizabeth pulled her shawl close around her waist and despite the chill (or maybe because of it), hurried down the narrow cobblestone street to a pier where several fish markets crowded in along a row of other tiny shops.

After her purchase was neatly wrapped and tucked under her arm, Elizabeth started up the hill, fully intending to go straight home where she knew her mama was waiting for that night's main course. But she couldn't seem to help herself.

The haunting sound of organ music and singing drew Elizabeth. She stopped and cocked her head, brushing strands of thick, shoulder-length brown hair away from her ear. The melody floated on the wind, apparently originating from one of the storefronts, and it seemed to call to her.

She moved toward it. This young girl loved music but never heard much of it at home, where life was hectic and endless chores didn't allow time for what her mother called "frivolity."

Opening the door just a crack, the young girl intended only to put her nose inside, but quickly her big brown eyes and the rest of her, including the fish, followed, and there she observed a strange sight.

Though Elizabeth was not accustomed to going to church, she recognized that this was indeed a chapel. High-backed wooden chairs were lined up in rows. In the front left corner a chubby little lady with curly gray hair strained to keep her feet pumping the air into a small pipe organ while her pudgy fingers played the keys to accompany those who were singing,

> Amazing grace! how sweet the sound,
> That saved a wretch like me![1]

Elizabeth slipped onto one of the chairs and placed her package carefully on the seat beside her as she looked around the dimly lit room. Occupying the hard, straight-backed seats were some of the most unlikely parishioners imaginable.

Here and there, big burly fishermen, some slouched over, some sitting tall and attentive, listened as the music trailed off and an old preacher opened his worn Bible and began delivering a passionate message about "the gospel that can save dark souls and set men free from sin and death."

At the end of his sermon, the minister pointed his finger around the room and asked, "Does anybody here want to receive Jesus today? Does anyone want to be set free?" Beckoning with his hand, he continued, "Then you must come forward and kneel down and pray, and the Lord Jesus will come into your heart and life."

Elizabeth was thinking about his words while one after the other, as if pulled by an unseen force, the unkempt fishermen stood and moved toward the preacher. Elizabeth certainly didn't want to miss anything, so she grabbed her fish and went and knelt at the old, wooden altar.

Kneeling beside her was a big brawny man with leathery skin. His head was bowed and tears were dribbling through his whiskered cheeks when a man came up behind him, squeezed his shoulder and said, "Pray on, brother."

So this smelly, wrinkled man looked up toward heaven and prayed in a husky voice: "Ooo Aw, Gawd! Deliver me from this ter-r-rrr-ble sin-a-drink!"

Elizabeth listened with interest. She watched the man's shoulders shake as he sobbed. Caught up in the power of that moment, she thought she ought to pray, but didn't know how. After a brief but determined silence she squeezed her eyes together, bowed her head, and said in her most solemn voice, "O, God, deliver me from this terrible sin of drink."

Somebody said, "Amen, sister." And the preacher smiled, because he knew what Elizabeth really meant.

And the organist played and sang:

> Down at the cross where my Savior died,
> Down where for cleansing from sin I cried,
> There to my heart was the blood applied;
> Glory to His name.[2]

Grandma Elizabeth—My Touchstone

All these years later, I'm so grateful that God understands the heart's desire and that He promises to satisfy the desires of our hearts. I'm thankful because He saved little Elizabeth that day. And as a twelve-year-old girl, my grandma went home and told her mother that she had invited the Lord Jesus into her heart and life.

Sadly, her mother didn't care. So, from that day on, that little Salvation Army church became Elizabeth's spiritual family. They raised her to love and serve the Lord. She knew she was saved from her sins though it took her a long time to grow in the Lord and to be able to articulate what had happened that Sunday afternoon on the way home from the fish market.

Many times when I've done things like sorting old photographs or family letters and keepsakes, memories of a godly grandma who was a prayer warrior flood my mind. Like the pearls on Ruth's keepsake box, those photo albums are a touchstone connecting me to Grandma Cowan, the cobblestone streets of England, and a little old preacher who introduced our family to the same God Joshua remembered at the Jordan River.

You Be the One

Maybe you don't have the memories I have of a grandma or a mother who decided to follow the Savior. If not, *you be the one!* You can decide right now to leave a spiritual legacy to those who will come after you. You don't need a chapel or a preacher or even fancy, elegant words. Just ask the God who knows your heart to begin a work in you and forgive your sins. Who knows? Someday your granddaughter may mention you in a book and bless you for the prayers and the memorials you planted in your family.

Thanks for the Memories

Sometimes I try to imagine what our family would have been like if Grandma Cowan hadn't experienced a miracle in a little storefront Salvation Army chapel. And I thank God for the memories of Mama, raised by that woman, to love and serve and give and do for others, and, most importantly, who prayed daily for her five daughters. Believe me, those prayers have made all the difference in my life.

I'm thankful for those touchstones and for the forgiveness they made possible. The Word of God says in Psalm 103 that the first benefit we can enjoy is having all our sins forgiven. We don't need to walk in doubt because as far as the east is from the west, so far has He removed all our sins from us. *Forgiven up-to-date* is God's plan for you and me.

How Do You Spell Relief?

"What happiness for those whose guilt has been forgiven!" the psalmist exclaimed. "What joys when sins are covered over! What relief for those who have confessed their sins and God has cleared their record" (Ps. 32:1-2 TLB).

How often I have identified with David's words: "There was a time when I wouldn't admit what a sinner I was. But my dishonesty made me miserable and filled my days with frustration. All day and all night your hand was heavy on me. My strength evaporated like water on a sunny day until I finally admitted all my sins to you and stopped trying to hide them. I said to myself, 'I will confess them to the Lord.' And you forgave me! All my guilt is gone" (Ps. 32:3-5 TLB).

He was really saying, "How do you spell relief? G-R-A-C-E!"

Lewis Smedes wrote, "Grace is the one word for all that God is for us in the form of Jesus Christ."[3] Grace is pardon for my sins no matter how unworthy I feel. That's why so many people call it *amazing* grace.

I remember that as a child I learned this little chorus:

> God has blotted them out!
> I'm happy and glad and free!
> God has blotted them out!
> I'll turn to Isaiah and see!
> Chapter forty-four, twenty-two and three,
> He's blotted them out! And now I can shout,
> For that means me!

God Doesn't Remember

Yesterday I felt the freshness of God's grace once again in a way that reminded me of that children's chorus and how it still applies. I struggle with a nagging sin. Its chronic presence sometimes leaves me feeling defeated. Just when I think I've got it under control, I carelessly slip up again.

Some might think it's no big deal. Some might say, "Daisy, you're being too hard on yourself." But a quiet, gentle voice always lets me know the truth. This sin makes me miserable.

Last week I did it again. I was having a phone conversation with a friend. We were talking about a third party and that's when it happened. I knew I didn't need to say it. It was true, but not uplifting. I shouldn't have shared it . . . but I did.

After we hung up, I tried to brush off the uneasy feeling sin leaves. But it washed over me in waves, leaving the salty taste of disobedience behind. I thought about how my friend would feel the next time she saw the woman I betrayed. The words were out. The damage was done. I couldn't take it back.

Picking up the phone, I punched my friend's number and quickly apologized for my careless tongue. Though she assured me the information had gone in one ear and out the other, I knew better. I remembered James 3:5: "The tongue is a small thing, but what enormous damage it can do" (TLB).

Alone with the Lord, I opened my Bible to Psalm 141:3 and prayed with the psalmist, "Help me, Lord, to keep my mouth shut and my lips sealed" (TLB).

Immediately I sensed again the awe of serving a Father who keeps no record of wrongs. Peter Gilquist, in his book *Love Is*

Now, has a wonderful word picture of what it means to be forgiven by God. Mr. Gilquist found himself frustrated with doing again and again what he wished he would not do. (Do you know the feeling? What hangs you up? gossip? bitterness? anger? guilt?) He was trusting in God's Word, but this silly habit kept rearing its ugly head.

He doesn't even identify the habit. It might have been something as innocuous to you and me as thinking ill of somebody, or maybe a careless word, or making fun of something that ought not to have been a joke.

Whatever the habit, he found wrenching misery in his repeated offense. He would go to the Lord, confess his sin, and receive assurance, both in his heart as well as from the Word that God did indeed forgive. But he felt discouraged. *Lord, how many times?* he groaned until he pictured himself on the top of a mountain getting as close as he could, and yelling to the skies, "God, I've done it again!"

And then, as if from the very throne room of heaven, he heard the voice of God say, "Done . . . *what?*"[4]

Forgiveness Is a Firm Foundation

It's not that the mighty God of the universe can't remember. He *chooses* forgetfulness toward our inadequacies. And no matter how vast our sins, God says, "I will remember them no more."

He can do that because His Son endured the Cross, standing between us and God, collecting our sins, screening out our blunders, presenting us pure before our heavenly Father. And we rejoice that God, in His great mercy, has given us new birth into a living hope through the resurrection of His Son, Jesus Christ, from the dead. What joy to cling to the living foundational memorial stone, Jesus Christ!

A Grace Box

One way I remember that God forgets my sin is by looking at one of my new "memorial stones." It is a beautiful, heart-shaped box that someone gave me. A scripted card accompanying the grace box reads:

> I will become a work of art
> Graciously created after God's own heart.
> The cardboard is covered with fabric, you see;
> Because of God's mercy, Christ's blood covers me!

When I lift the lid on that decorative heart, the grace box is empty — reminding me that my sins have disappeared because of Christ.

Again and again in my own life I need to remember that His forgiveness is as available as my next breath. I need to apply 1 John 1:9, "If we confess our sins, He is faithful and just to forgive us our sins and to cleanse us from all unrighteousness."

I need to apply that truth often and sincerely agree with God that I am, in fact, in need of forgiveness. And regularly I need to remember the Cross and to reflect on the resurrection of hope. That's why the grace box is a memorial stone I keep on the coffee table in plain view.

But that's not enough. After everything else, I need also to listen for that mystical, renewing word from God that washes over me and is such a joyous relief when He says, "Daisy, you say you've done it again?

"Done . . . *what?*"

Memo to myself:
    —*Dust our photo albums*
    —*Write a letter to Emily Elizabeth reminding her of her great-great-grandmother, whose name she bears . . . and of her heritage of grace*

Prayer:
    Thank You, Lord, for those who so convincingly showed me the way. Thank You for the benefit of Your amazing grace, and may I behave as Your beneficiary. Amen.

Before I forget—I'll do it today:
    What reminders of forgiveness can you place around your home?
    What habit causes you grief today? Confess it, now. Whenever the guilt rises up today, remember—it's dealt with and forgotten.

$\mathcal{H}$e Remembers to Heal Us

Who heals all your diseases. . . .
(Ps. 103:3)

$\mathcal{H}$ave you ever gotten one of those calls — one you expected but never felt ready for?

Mama was dying. My sister called, telling me to come east quickly. I phoned the airlines. As I tossed clothes and necessities into a suitcase, memories floated in and out of my heart . . . memories of a mama who taught me to be grateful and to trust; memories of a mama who constantly cared for others, especially her husband and five daughters; memories of a mama who was always strong and healthy, who laughed a lot and cried when she had to and taught us the importance of prayer by her example. You can probably imagine how I felt when I saw her later that day.

Our Bodies Embarrass Us

When I arrived in New Jersey and saw this little woman curled up in her hospital bed, looking so tiny and defenseless, I thought she didn't even resemble the mama I knew and loved all these years. The one who always battled being too heavy. The one who was so modest. The one who, in recent years, still tried to keep up with chores and schedules and became so disgusted when she just wasn't getting the mileage out of her body she used to.

Mama certainly understood what the apostle Paul was saying back in the first century when he wrote, "The bodies we now have embarrass us for they become sick and die; but they will be full of glory when we come back to life again. Yes, they are weak, dying bodies now, but when we live again they will be full of strength" (1 Cor. 15:43 TLB).

Mama's dying body often embarrassed her. She once planned a trip to visit my sister Emily in Philadelphia. Since Daddy had stopped driving for safety reasons, Mama traveled on a Greyhound bus. During the trip she started to feel sick and when the bus arrived unusually early, Mama realized that Emily probably wouldn't be there to meet her. As she stepped down and away from the door of the bus a wave of dizziness washed over her, and Mama fainted away on the bus station floor.

Apparently one of the station attendants saw her go down and rushed over to offer assistance. Kneeling beside her, he pushed the visor on his cap back and bent down to listen to Mama's heart. Then, leaning even closer, he put his face right in front of hers, probably to determine if she was breathing.

Mama said that was precisely when she came around, startled to see this strange man with round, apple cheeks staring right in her face, their noses almost touching. Blinking a couple of times, she gathered her wits enough to voice the most important thought in her mind at the moment.

"Mister?" she asked, and then paused so she could form the words just right. "Is my dress pulled down?" The man raised his eyebrows, bent backward, glancing toward her feet and answered slowly, in a nasal kind of a tone. "You look very nice, lady."

The Touchstone of Healing

When the psalmist wrote He "heals all your diseases," Mama Guldenschuh knew full well that he wasn't talking about the old, worn-out frame that wasn't serving her too well anymore. Just before Mama went to heaven, we wheeled Daddy into the room. For me, the hardest part about Mama's dying was Daddy. For the nearly sixty-two years of their married life he had provided for her. Even now he made sure that bills were paid and that she'd be cared for when he was gone. It never occurred to him that God would take Mama first. It would be hard seeing him alone.

We pulled his wheelchair close to the bed. Daddy reached for Mama's hand. With her other hand she motioned weakly for my four sisters and me to crowd around her as she breathed a deep sigh of satisfaction that we were all finally there.

Then, to our amazement, she looked right at Emily and in a strong voice declared, "Emily — the Balloon Lady!" We laughed a bit nervously.

"Doris — the Delft plate!" she continued. We were starting to catch on. "Ruth — the Hummel angel."

Mama was doling out her earthly treasures. Then, the last thing she did was look up at us with her eyes wide open.

"Sing!" she commanded, then pointed a finger at my older sister, who is a pastor's wife, and at me and said firmly, "But you two, don't sing!" (Mama hadn't lost her musical sense! My parents always teasingly said, "Daisy was really cut out to be a musician . . . they just sewed her up wrong!" or "Daisy always had a lot of music in her, but none ever came out!")

Nevertheless, we sang around Mama's bed as best we could the lovely song she requested:

> Because He lives, I can face tomorrow.
> Because He lives, all fear is gone.
> Because I know He holds the future,
> Life is worth the living just because He lives.[1]

When we finished, Mama looked up and said, "Now sing 'O that will be glory for me, glory for me, glory for me; when by His grace I shall look on his face, that will be glory, be glory for me!' "[2]

The psalmist says, "What a benefit! He heals all my diseases." My mama knew. The most glorious touchstone in Scripture is the reminder that God does, indeed, heal all our diseases when He welcomes us into the throne room of heaven. Mama entered God's presence with singing.

All My Diseases?

Yet there are some who would complain, "Wait just a minute! I've got these pains in my chest [or cancer or a sore throat or a thousand other problems]. He does not heal *all* my diseases."

"Because He Lives." Words by William J. and Gloria Gaither. Music by William J. Gaither. © Copyright 1971 by William J. Gaither. All rights reserved. Used by permission.

One woman told me she had an Excedrin-headache for three weeks. "How come I'm not healed?"

Berniece faces daily the severe pain of crippling arthritis in her spine. So many other friends have undergone the anguish of a mastectomy. I've struggled with a myriad of female problems. Once I spent three days in the hospital to undergo yet another breast biopsy.

I'm thankful to report it was benign. Yet the healing for me was not in the verdict, but in the absence of fear. What about you? What are you struggling with? Are you fighting fatigue? a virus? Maybe you have a broken ankle.

Perhaps it's far more serious. You were shocked to test positive for HIV when you weren't in a high-risk group. Your doctor called you in to say the lump they removed last Tuesday was malignant. Or maybe you're watching your husband or child grapple with the aftereffects of a tragic accident.

You're not alone. We all whisper that same question at one time or another. *Why me? Why doesn't God heal me?*

What's the answer? What does it take to feel the benefit of God's healing power? More than anything I believe it involves our chosen response to God's purpose in our lives. It involves yielding our will and trusting His goodness, no matter the cost. Experiencing His healing requires an attitude that says, "Lord, I offer You a sacrifice of thanksgiving, that You might be honored by my response to what the world calls unfairness."

A healing of the heart and inner life comes for one who can say, "What a benefit! He heals all my diseases and I have been freed from shaking my fist in the face of God and demanding: 'Why have You not corrected this situation?' " Oh, what a benefit. What inner healing.

Grave Stones

Maybe we could call this memorial stone a *grave* stone because it represents the dying of self. I say this after hearing a man whose attitude toward personal suffering revolutionized my thought process on what it means to be healed according to Psalm 103.

Charlie Weidemeyer is the football coach for Los Gatos High School in California near San Jose. Charlie was diagnosed with Lou Gehrig's disease and given only three years to live — fifteen years ago. Since then Charlie's disease has progressed and he has been confined to a wheelchair. In fact, he is strapped to it.

Not long ago one of the major television networks made a two-hour, prime-time movie based on Charlie Weidemeyer's life. It dramatized how he is slowly losing all of his functions, including his voice. Inside, he is a brilliant individual. However, his speech is discernable only to his wife and an assistant, who accompany him everywhere and interpret his eye movements and read his lips. For Charlie, communicating is a painstaking process.

Incredibly, through these two faithful attendants, Charlie has continued to coach the football team at least part time. He still serves in that capacity because of his knowledge of the game and because he is such a catalyst for the spirit of the school and the team.

When interviewed recently on a talk show, Charlie was asked a question that he must have heard a million times.

"Charlie, you're a religious man. Do you pray to be healed?"

I can't express to you the impact on my life when, through his wife, and with sparkling, clear eyes, Charlie Weidemeyer answered, "I have been healed of the need to be healed." [3]

God Remembers What We Are

Now, that is freedom. Pure. True. No strings. Freedom. To say with the psalmist, "He heals all my diseases." *All* of them. It is profound. All the things that would keep me so earthbound; all the things that are making me depend on this shell of a body: "I've been healed of the need."

Is it time to ball up your fist and beat the air and scream about the inequities of life? Or can you open that hand and ask if there's still time to coach a football team from your wheelchair?

When I was a young married woman I had to ask myself that kind of a question. How desperately David and I wanted children. After years of medical tests, hopes lifted and dashed, then finally a necessary hysterectomy, I asked, "Why?" but with the help of my husband's strong faith, we opened our hands, our hearts, and our home.

We worked with dependent and neglected children in a Salvation Army home, crying with the abused, binding wounded emotions, and finally God allowed us to adopt our own two precious children. All these years later I am reminded: Diseases are temporary. Souls are permanent.

My mama went to glory quite awhile before Ruth designed the special keepsake box. I need only to touch Mama's pearls on the lid to remind me that our bodies aren't us. Mama couldn't be contained in that unreliable frame — that embarrassing body.

Now I understand what Paul meant when he wrote to the church at Corinth and to us about our earthly forms.

> They are just human bodies at death, but when they come back to life they will be superhuman bodies. For just as there are natural, human bodies, there are also supernatural, spiritual bodies. . . . First, then, we have these human bodies and later on God gives us spiritual, heavenly bodies. Adam was made from the dust of the earth, but Christ came from heaven above. Every human being has a body just like Adam's, made of dust, but all who become Christ's will have the same kind of body as his — a body from heaven.
>
> (1 Cor. 15:44, 46-48 TLB)

How Do You Heal Dust?

Psalm 103:14 assures me, "For He knows our frame; He remembers that we are dust." What a benefit! He remembers what we really are. Some of us are dustier than others! Someone told me of a little boy whose mother told him to wash up for dinner. "Oh, Mom," he whined, "can't you just dust me?"

But, really. Think about it. You and me? We're dust! What difference does it make if dust is rearranged? But if our *attitudes* are healed, that's for eternity.

Remember to Be Free

We need to pray that the Lord will heal us from the need to have perfected bodies this side of heaven. I laughed when a friend gave me a copy of a "Loretta" cartoon. It says that Loretta doesn't use wrinkle cream anymore — she just overeats to keep her skin tight!

The older I get, the more I pay attention to that kind of comedy. Especially in a commercialized world where we're expected to stay young and perfect. Maybe if we could remember, as God does, that our bodies are only a glob of moist dust, we could be free from the unrealistic, unhealthy expectations of this carnal environment.

Yes, our bodies embarrass us, but we can laugh because we're looking forward to future victory. There's something wonderfully liberating about being able to say, "I've been healed from the need to be healed." And I'm not lingering on this side of glory begging, "Lord, You've got to fix this thing in my chest and the bump on my toe. I deserve that."

Remembering What's Important

In the 1800s, a clergyman named Albert B. Simpson launched a vibrant ministry of evangelism and Bible teaching in England that spread all over the world. A.B. Simpson must have had a handle on Psalm 103 and the freedom of maturing to a point of understanding true healing. I love what he wrote:

> Once it was the blessing, now it is the Lord;
> Once it was the feeling, now it is His Word.
> Once His gift I wanted, now the Giver own;
> Once I sought for healing; now Himself alone.[4]

A.B. Simpson knew that true healing comes when we want God more than anything earthly.

Memo to myself:
  Remember to take my medicine
  — Do my exercise
  — Take supper to neighbors recovering from the flu
  —and sit awhile

Prayer:
  Lord, I feel so good today! Please be with my friend who is facing yet another chemotherapy session and its aftermath. Thank You for Your healing power in body and soul. Amen.

Before I forget—I'll do it today:
  What "diseases," physical or emotional, continually get between you and God?
  How can you begin to say of them, "I've been healed of the need to be healed"?
  What small step can you take toward acceptance today?

Chapter 4

Satisfaction Guaranteed

[He] satisfies your mouth with good things,
So that your youth is renewed like the eagle's.
(Ps. 103:5)

I guess you could call it an unearthly escapade — or maybe an *uplifting* experience. Nevertheless, in January last year I had an adventure.

I often receive invitations that give me the privilege of traveling and speaking all over the country and sometimes overseas. How would you feel if someone expected your presence in a place you never knew existed?

"Daisy, would you come to Adak?"

"Well, I might be inclined to," I told the Navy base chaplain, "if I had any idea where it is!"

Beautiful Downtown Adak

He informed me that Adak is three islands away from Siberia on the Aleutian Chain. That certainly clarified things for me.

Legally, Adak is part of Alaska and there are five thousand American Navy personnel on that tiny island in the north Pacific.

It never occurred to me, as I located a blank space on my calendar and penciled in the engagement, that flying through Anchorage on a small plane with a bush pilot to a tiny island that is probably the farthest civilized place to the west and that just happens to be nicknamed "the birthplace of the winds," might be a harrowing experience.

Before we took off on the appointed date I looked at a map.

I found my magnifying glasses and looked again.

I Don't Want to Go!

"Lord," this white-knuckled flyer prayed, "will we ever find it?"

As it turned out, we blew over it! Adak's nickname was accurate. As we neared it, the pilot announced nonchalantly, "Well, folks, conditions for landing are below our safety standards."

Would you be nervous? "Great," I thought. "We're only four hundred miles from Siberia. Why not land there?" I was fretting . . . January. Windy. Alaska. Freezing. Siberia. *What am I doing here?*

The pilot interrupted my worries to inform us we'd probably be landing in Shimeya. Why didn't that make me feel safer?

"Oh, Shim-m-m-eee-yah," I said out loud. "Sure. That'll be just fine." I was fairly certain the Lord would still receive my prayer signals from Shimeya.

Maybe the name of the place has something to do with it, but the powerful air current made us feel like the plane was shimmying in for a landing. When conditions were safer we made our way back to Adak where we almost landed sideways — the wind was so strong. I was just glad to be on the ground again.

Rising Above the Ordinary

A chaplain's assistant met me at the airport to escort me to the assigned quarters and that's when I saw the most amazing thing. We were just driving along when, there on a dirty metal garbage Dumpster, perched as regally as you please, was an American eagle.

"Would you please look over there?" I gasped and grabbed the man's arm so excitedly he almost lost the wheel.

His response disappointed me.

"Yeah. Uh-huh," he mumbled in a so-what tone.

The next instant I saw another one. Then another one. I had never been that close to so many eagles. They were everywhere.

"It's no big deal," the assistant explained. "We have about three hundred eagles on Adak, and they're a real nuisance. Scavengers. When we try to have a barbecue, they come and steal all our meat!"

A New Perspective

After my short stay on the island of Adak, I can now tell you more about American eagles than you want to know. But it was certainly interesting to study how they live and to understand for the first time what it really means to be renewed like the eagles (see Ps. 103:5).

Eagles fly higher than any other bird. And they fly alone. They mate for life, and the happy couple builds a nest designed to endure.

First, they find a crevice in one of the rocky crags of a mountain because there are no trees in the natural terrain. In fact, Adak is so bare that a number of years ago some Navy men planted about a dozen pine trees near the airport. A sign there reads: *You are now entering and leaving the Adak National Forest!*

Have you ever been amazed by the practical lessons you can learn from nature? God speaks to us through nature. He spoke to me through the eagles. The eagle's nest is like my life. The eagle creates his large nest by gathering stones, driftwood, or whatever sturdy objects are available. Most are sharp and coarse.

Often life's events are like that. We grow through the rough times.

But then the eagle adds skins and furs of animals like rabbits or mice to downy feathers to cover up the rough, hard edges and create a soft bed for the family. The eggs are hatched and the mother eagle cares for her young, bringing them food and keeping them warm. They trust her and wait patiently in the nest for their next meal.

Those Feathers Have Got to Go!

God often does that for us. He shelters us from the trials of life until He knows it's time for us to grow.

But then comes the day when the eaglets are no longer small enough to be dependent. It's time for them to learn to fly. Not surprisingly, they don't want to go. They are loathe to move out of their comfort zone.

Wisely, the mother and father begin to remove the soft cushions from the nest. They pluck out the lining until the sharp rocks and sticks are exposed beneath the downy softness.

The young eagles become uncomfortable. They are being trained by hardship. It's part of growing up. When God spoke through the prophet Isaiah about being renewed and soaring like eagles, He acknowledged that it is the weak who need strengthening.

Listen to His words:

> He gives power to the weak,
> And to those who have no might He increases strength.
> Even the youths shall faint and be weary,
> And the young men shall utterly fall,
> But those who wait on the Lord
> Shall renew their strength;
> They shall mount up with wings like eagles,
> They shall run and not be weary,
> They shall walk and not faint.
>   (Isa. 40:29-31)

Now I know what it really means to be renewed like eagles. It means first I must be weary. Do you relate to these words: tired? weak? faint? The Lord seems to be saying, "Daisy, I'll help you mount up with wings — even though I removed the comfort zone. That's part of My plan. I am with you and I'll show you how to fly high and to move above the circumstances. Then you'll grow. You will become all I had in mind for you to be."

It would be much easier to just stay in a protected, comfortable place. But the Father says, "No, I've called you. I have in mind that you will soar. That you will mount up with wings. Sometimes you'll fly high. Sometimes you'll fly alone."

Manufacturer's Guarantee

When you purchase a new piece of furniture or clothing or a gift for a friend, you expect quality. Often advertisers guarantee the consumer's satisfaction.

Wouldn't we be disappointed if we got our product home from the marketplace and discovered flaws and broken places? What if our plush new couch was delivered and we sat on exposed rocks and twigs?

The satisfaction the world offers is different from the kind God promises in Psalm 103:5. God's promise is to satisfy my desires with *good* things. Are good things always comfortable?

The most common trap we fall into is that of comparing ourselves to others. If a friend or neighbor has a nicer house, car, boat, job, family, I may feel dissatisfied. Yet the things God sees as good are the things that make me grow, not necessarily the things that make me comfortable.

One of Wall Street's biggest success secrets is keeping consumers dissatisfied while promising contentment with the purchase of one more product. Every television or magazine ad strives to make the viewer discontented. Bombarded with other people's ideas about what is *good*, it's easy to lose direction. In fact it becomes a temptation to feather our nest instead of growing out of it to finally soar with eagle's wings.

In a recent issue of *Today's Christian Woman*, author Annie Chapman suggested five ways to avoid being caught up in discontent:

1.   Take the focus off yourself.
2.   Call it what it is: coveting (sin).
3.   Count your blessings.
4.   Keep your eyes on the eternal.
5.   Pray for portion control.[1]

I would add one more:

6.   Desire what God wants for you.

When the Lord promises to satisfy my desires, He refers to a satisfaction that doesn't produce apathy. Secular satisfaction is a fleeting thing and, frankly, very relative.

Spiritual satisfaction keeps us moving. We can capture the paradox of the eagle's nest if we pray, "Lord, keep me forever unsatisfied." The good things are often the rocks and sticks. They are what move us to mount up with wings.

When I'm tempted to seek the satisfaction of the world, I remember: TDCRW. It's from Psalm 37:

> *Trust* in the LORD. . . .
> *Delight* yourself also in the LORD,
> And He shall give you the desires of your heart.
>
> *Commit* your way to the LORD. . . .
> *Rest* in the LORD, and *wait* patiently for Him.
> (Ps. 37:3-7)

TDCRW. Satisfaction guaranteed.

Memo to myself:
   —Update my wish list—after checking Philippians 4:11-13
   — Remember that_____
was so satisfying, and keep on learning to be content . . .
even as I grow older
Prayer:

The years are slipping by, dear Lord. Keep me young in heart, and dissatisfied with anything short of You. Amen.

Before I forget—I'll do it today:
   What soft cushions has God removed from your nest? Are you hesitating to fly?
   What sharp rocks and sticks are pushing you?
   Is it time to go?
   How can you begin—today?
   What stands between you and satisfaction? Be honest—do you really need it? How can you practice being satisfied today?

Chapter 5

What's a Guldenschuh?

I will not forget you.
See, I have inscribed you on the palms of My hands.
(Isa. 49:15-16)

*W*hat's your favorite flower?
Guess what mine is! Most people think of a daisy as the symbol of innocence and sweetness. Adolescent peers found it necessary to remind me often that daisies are weeds.

So I was very insecure about my name. Together with my last name, *Guldenschuh*, which is pronounced "Golden Shoe," it became fodder for a lot of teasing. I was often "Tulip Silver Slipper" or some other floral combination.

Eventually I shook off any negative insinuations about my name. In fact, now that I'm more seasoned I capitalize on it by wearing daisy pins and earrings and buying fabrics with a daisy print.

I think it's lovely when someone gives me a bunch of daisies or sings that old song, "A Bicycle Built for Two," as if I've never heard it before. It gives me name recognition. That's important because our names say a lot about who we are. We feel accepted when someone recognizes our name.

What Did You Say Your Name Was?

Did you ever forget to take your name tag off after a Tupperware party or a Sunday school gathering? Lou Ann stopped at a grocery store after a morning Bible study. At the check-out stand the good-humored clerk said, "Lou Ann, it's so good to see you! I've been wondering how you were doing — haven't seen ya in a long time!"

Not realizing she had this big three-by-five card pinned to her shoulder, Lou Ann scratched her head, smiling, trying for all the world to remember this person she thought she'd never met before.

Did you ever try to pretend to know someone you really don't remember?

Finally, she had to admit it. "What did you say your name was?"

The clerk roared with laughter. "Gotcha!" he giggled. "Do you always wear your name tag when you shop?"

God Remembers My Name

Our names are personal. They are one of our most treasured possessions. When our son, David, left for college, I noticed that one of the first things he packed in his suitcase was a name plaque we had given him.

When someone remembers your name, you feel significant and cared for. In biblical times a person's name was of vast importance. When a baby was born, the parents would ponder and pray, trying to choose a name that would be big enough for their tiny son or daughter to grow into. Every name had a specific meaning. A name was a challenge. It was a symbol of hopes and dreams and everything that person could become.

"O Lord, you have examined my heart and know everything about me..." the shepherd king's thoughts are recorded in Psalm 139. "Every moment you know where I am.... I can never be lost to your Spirit! I can *never* get away from my God!" (Ps. 139:1-8 TLB).

Time and again God promises, "I will never forget you" (see Isa. 49:15-16). He knows us so intimately that the hairs on our heads are numbered (though I must admit it's hard to imagine the usefulness of that information!). God remembers who we are. We are carved in the palm of His hand.

How do you feel knowing God can never forget your name?

Three Names That Start With "B"

We lived in Puerto Rico when our son was in first grade at the Mennonite Academy. Every day I met him at the bus stop after school.

This particular day, David had hurriedly stuffed a stack of school papers into my hand and then darted off in the direction of our home. "What's the rush?" I yelled as I took a minute to flip through the papers.

"David, wait a minute! You picked up some other person's papers by mistake!"

David ran back to me and, with assurance, put his hands on his hips and stuck his little chin out. In the blue and white uniform of the academy he looked like a tiny executive ready to make his case.

"Those are my papers," he stated despite the fact that I showed him the large letters scrawled across the top of each page: R-O-D-R-I-Q-U-E-Z.

"My name is now Rodriquez. I don't want to be David Hepburn anymore. I'm David Rodriquez."

I was worried for a moment. What could make our young son want to desert his family?

"None of my friends can say 'Hepburn,' " David explained. "They can pronounce 'Rodriquez' real good. But everyone makes fun of Hepburn. So I want to be David Rodriquez, okay?"

Then I understood. Here we were in a place where everyone used a different language. David's best friends were twins, Jaime and Damaris Rodriquez. David wanted to belong. He wanted a name that would roll off the tongue and trill dramatically like the names of his Puerto Rican friends.

When you think about it, David's experience isn't that unique, is it? How important it is for each of us to have a sense of belonging.

The apostle Paul said, "Now, therefore, you are no longer strangers and foreigners, but fellow citizens with the saints and members of the household of God, having been built on the foundation of the apostles and prophets, Jesus Christ Himself being the chief cornerstone" (Eph. 2:19-20).

What a wonderful thing it is to belong. I'm a member of God's forever family, and I do not have to wonder if I have been accepted. God has named me *Belonging*.

I remember another time when our young David arrived home from his seventh-grade class with the sting of a severe reprimand by the principal of the school. He had been punished for misbehaving and as most mothers would, I felt sorry for him.

We were seated around the supper table later that day and in my overzealous attempt to quiet his fears and build security in him I went on and on with encouraging words. Though he certainly would have to pay his debt to society and to the school for misbehaving, I assured him there was nothing he could do that could ever make us love him less.

"No matter what happens, David," I told him rather dramatically, "we will always stand by you. You are very precious to us, and I want you to remember this: Your name means 'beloved.' We want you to understand that you are beloved of God and beloved of all of us."

While he was giving me that unique adolescent "enough-is-enough" look I heard our eight-year-old mumble something as she looked down into her plate.

"What did you say, honey?"

She paused for a moment before looking up. "I said, 'I wish my name meant *beloved*!' "

And I can hearken back to the giggle my husband and I shared as we said in unison, "Your name is 'Beloved,' too!"

Can you think of anything more precious than someone calling you "Beloved"? King David was born into a situation where his first job was that of an ordinary shepherd boy. But his mother, with prayer and probably fasting, and much soul-searching, had given him a name that means "beloved of God."

Reading the Old Testament, I realized that most of the people in Israel were surprised when Samuel anointed David, the young shepherd, to become king. Yet as David followed God, growing in wisdom, stumbling sometimes, but always getting back up, he became what his name implied. The Bible calls David "a man after God's own heart." Generations now know that God referred to David as "My beloved." That's what was inscribed on our son's name plaque: "David, beloved of God."

Besides the fact that my husband's name is David, that definition is the reason we chose our son's name. He was only three days old when I held that beautiful, chosen (adopted) baby for the first time. As I rocked and cuddled him I remember thinking, "David! Oh, what a wonderful name for our son! Every single day of his life as he writes it or when someone speaks it he will be reminded that he is truly beloved of God."

God has named us *Belonging* because we are His. He has named us *Beloved* and there is nothing we can do to make Him love us less. But there is another name perhaps more important than any other.

Years ago in a Salvation Army home for unwed mothers a teenaged girl was fascinated by the sweet spirit of the nurses and said to one of them, "Why do nurses wear white?"

It wasn't a question she had been asked before, but after a minute the nurse answered, "White signifies the purity of our profession."

As she pondered her future and her past, dark remembrances swept the lonely mother-to-be. She asked with a quiet, quivering voice, "Will I ever be able to wear white?"

The nurse wrapped her arms around that young woman and wisely responded, "Oh yes. Yes, dear, you can wear white — because God is able."

Isaiah 61:10 (TLB) gives us the picture of the bride being adorned and prepared.

> I will greatly rejoice in the Lord,
> My soul shall be joyful in my God;

> For He has clothed me with the garments of salvation,
> He has covered me with the robe of righteousness,
> As a bridegroom decks himself with ornaments,
> And as a bride adorns herself with her jewels.

In a New Testament wedding story (Matt. 22) Jesus tells about someone who arrives without wedding clothes. The parable is about our opportunity (which is the most rational thing we could choose) — to exchange the false righteousness of our own filthy rags for the robe of His righteousness. By our personal choice we avail ourselves of the pure wedding garment and appropriate His great grace.

By our choice and His power He names you and me *Blameless*, not because we're not guilty, but because there's nothing that He holds against us anymore. Hallelujah! "Yes, My child, you can wear white!"

> Purer in heart, O God, Help me to be;
> That I Thy holy face one day may see.
> Keep me from secret sin,
> Reign Thou my soul within;
> Purer in heart, O God, help me to be.
> Anna Davison

Ephesians 1:3-6 reveals that God *chose* us to be blameless. In love He adopted us into His family in accordance with His pleasure and His perfect will, to the praise of His glorious grace.

Named for His Forever Family

I am the mother of chosen children and very unashamedly

pro-life. I have had the privilege of living out in my own home in a tangible way the truth Paul described when he said, "Long ago, even before he made the world, God chose us to be his very own, through what Christ would do for us; he decided then to make us holy in his eyes, without a single fault — we who stand before him covered with his love" (Eph. 1:4 TLB).

We were in the judge's chambers. Our new baby girl was two months old and had already been dedicated to the Lord at church. I had our whole family dolled up because I wanted to look just perfect (and impress the judge). Four-year-old David had his hair slicked back and was wearing one of the popular Eton jackets that were in style. I had made it especially for this occasion.

"Do you realize the gravity of why you are here?" The judge addressed my husband as we finalized the adoption proceedings.

"From this moment on, she is yours. You will be responsible for her education. She will be the beneficiary of all you own. You will be legally accountable to provide for her, protect her. . . ." He went on and on.

Of course we were willing, joyfully, to agree. But then the judge turned to our son. He must have seemed like a big, dark tower.

"Do you realize this little girl is your sister? From now on you are responsible to protect her and defend her. If anyone ever picks on her it's up to you to help her and be her big brother, do you understand?"

At age four, David was more concerned with just getting out of there than about making deep, lifelong commitments! With the fear of God in his eyes, he nodded furiously the whole time the judge was questioning him and punctuated each nod with a squeaky, "Yes! Yes! Yes! Yes!"

That day was a turning point as it is in each of our lives when we seal a relationship. Whether it's at a marriage altar or when a baby is handed to us, the idea is that we willingly, joyfully — but with eyes wide open — enter into the responsibility of the relationship.

Though God names us *Blameless*, there are certain spiritual guidelines as to what this relationship involves. We are unable to fulfill our part of the bargain, unable to do and be all that Scripture says or all the name "Christian" implies.

To bear the name of Christ and to say that because I have knowingly accepted the relationship as well as the responsibilities, do you feel as I do? "Lord, without You more than fulfilling Your part of the bargain, I'll never make it!"

He comforts, "You belong to My family."

Isaiah 43:1 says, "I have called you by your name; / You are Mine."

God is saying, "You're precious. Honored. I love you. You belong to Me." That's enough for me!

We named our little girl Lois because I never met a Lois I didn't love. I thought of every Lois I've known who has made a difference in my life and how wonderful it would be if our little girl grew to be like one of these godly women I knew.

The spiritual significance of the name Lois is "victorious." In the book of Acts as well as 1 Timothy, Lois is mentioned as Timothy's grandmother. I pictured the time that Paul perhaps came knocking on the door of Lois and Eunice's home, saying, "Is there anybody in this house who is ready to go and serve the Lord?"

What a thrill it must have been for Lois to say "Here he is! This is my grandson, and his mother, Eunice, and I have taught him the things of the Lord." That is our heart's desire for our Lois. That she would be the kind of mother and grandmother expecting her children to serve the Lord and then doing her part to get them ready!

Señor Martinez

We once met a man named Jesus Martinez, shortly after he entered into a personal relationship with the One for whom he was named. We marveled at the ways he tried to honor that name and grow into the person God wanted him to be.

Occasionally I think about a mother a long time ago — eighty years ago — tucked away in a mountain village in Puerto Rico, who bore a little son and gave him that name, probably hoping and praying he would grow to be like that One.

There is no other name above the name of Jesus. I was reminded again with a smile while standing next to a lady at a retreat. We were all singing that wonderful song of worship and praise, "Jesus, Name Above All Names," and my friend was giggling the whole time and I thought "My goodness." I couldn't wait to ask her what was so funny about this song. Was it the pianist? The circumstances? The woman in front of her?

"I can't sing that song anymore without laughing," she told me later, "for I stood next to my almost-four-year-old in church a few weeks ago and heard him singing at the top of his lungs: 'Jesus, name above ball games. . . .' "

I think he had great theology and knew something about priorities, for a four-year-old!

Memos to myself:
    — *Look up the meaning of our family's names*
    — *Make each a plaque, choosing a great scripture (a good time to practice my calligraphy)*
    — *Get new name tags for Bible study*

Prayer:
    Lord, help me to make everyone in our family—for that matter, everyone in Bible study—feel like they belong—because they do! Amen.

Before I forget—I'll do it today:
    Do you like your name? If not, how can you begin to associate good things with it? Think of five good things about yourself and say them out loud: (your name) is _____.
    How can you remind yourself that God calls you Beloved, Belonging, Blameless?

Chapter 6

The Love Gift

He remembers His covenant forever,
The word which He commanded, for a thousand generations.
(Ps. 105:8)

"*D*aisy, do we dare take this risk?"

I was receiving phone calls from all over the city. Actually, it was a miracle that telephones were even working. Thousands of aftershocks rocked the rolling hills, winding streets, and rushing waves of the San Francisco Bay Area. It was the day after the 7.1 earthquake I described earlier. Many in the community were edgy if not fearful about what might happen next.

Should we go on with the dailiness of ordinary living? Should we pack up, head for the airport, and fly away? Should we cancel commitments? Sit tight? Move on? Hibernate? What would you do?

If the Roof Falls In

No one knew. And so we decided to go ahead and do it. We would risk having Morning Break, our Bible study and weekly gathering for mental and spiritual health. Bridgemont, the old,

52

ornate Gothic-looking convent which now houses a Christian high school, would hopefully still be structurally sound and safe for our fellowship and Bible study.

The sixty brave ladies who ventured out to bond together that day amazed me. Who could be sure the roof wouldn't fall in? No one could promise it wouldn't. We were all on shaky ground. But, surprisingly, they came. And even more surprisingly, they were changed that Thursday morning by a secret promise, one God had prepared uniquely for that particular week, that day, that moment—before the foundation of our quivering world was even laid.

Have you ever experienced a time when your world seemed to be crumbling right under your feet? Some seasons of life can be like internal earthquakes. Nobody warned you about the "big one" that was about to hit. Someone betrayed you, a loved one died, you lost your financial security, or a relationship failed. Maybe the doctor said, "The tests came back positive," and your emotional Richter Scale measured 7.1.

But in the waves of aftershock, did you hear a whisper? A hope? A promise? And, were you surprised?

It was like that for me—maybe for all of us at Morning Break. The hostesses were a bit nervous as they shook out the red and white checkered tablecloths and turned over coffee cups. Someone noticed a new crack in the high, dome-shaped, plaster ceiling. We chose not to dwell on impending danger.

The Love Gift

We needed each other. So we began by rehashing what we'd been through. Feeling responsible to lift spirits and get things rolling, I grabbed the microphone and therapeutically shared a detailed account of my whereabouts at 5:04 p.m. on October 17th. Don't you think everyone was curious about how it feels to be stuck in your bathtub while your house is falling down around you?

After several ladies shared, we prayed, sang choruses, and arrived at the appointed time for our Love Gift, a weekly ceremony to bring encouragement and comfort to one another.

I adopted that idea from a church in Tucson, Arizona, where the women use it regularly as part of C.A.R.E. (Christ's Arms Reaching Everyone). Each week one lady will give a Love Gift to someone in the group. The gift is something significant to her; more than just a door prize, something from her heart. In advance, the giver prays for the recipient, asking God to customize the gift and make it something she will need or want.

I cannot express to you how moved I was when the woman in Tucson gave as her Love Gift a loaf of homemade bread and reminisced about the way her mother used to fill their home with the aroma of love. With a hug she passed along this prayed-over specialty to a woman who was a newcomer in Tucson and really needed that tender touch of home.

The Love Gift tradition at Morning Break has come to mean a lot to all of us. But never more than on October 19, 1989. That's when it was Patty's turn.

The Secret Promise

She stood up and her lip quivered slightly. "I have known for two weeks that this would be my turn to give the Love Gift. God gave me a melody to a verse of Scripture a few weeks ago. As I prepared, I thought my song would be my gift, and then I made a tape of praise songs and decided to choose a woman who needs encouragement. Maybe someone whose world is falling apart."

Huddled together, in our hearts we all felt, "I'm that woman!"

Patty could not have known how prophetic her song was. She lifted her soft, sweet voice and sang these words:

> God is our refuge and strength, an ever present help in
>   trouble.
> Therefore we will not fear, though the earth give way and
>   the mountains fall into the heart of the sea,
> though its waters roar and foam and the mountains quake
>   with their surging.
>
> (Ps. 46:1-3 NIV)

Can you believe it? Who but God could have orchestrated a moment in time like that? A holy hush fell over our group. We had been given a Divine Love Gift. A precious reminder of an age-old truth: *God is utterly dependable.*

His promise was as intimately personal to us as it must have been to the one who penned it centuries ago. Therefore we — in the city by the Bay — will not fear. Though the earth quake — even if it's the Big One — though the earth give way (TV news experts have told us this was not the Big One) — God, who remembers to keep His promises, is *completely* faithful.

How Could I Forget?

Though a thousand generations pass, He never forgets. Listen, do you need a place of refuge? Are the mountains of problems and disappointments quaking around you? Are you looking for a safe place to escape? Here's an important reminder: Your secret hiding place can be found at the altar of your heart if the God who remembers to keep His promises dwells there.

My friend Lou Ann often tells women in the midst of their hardship to keep in mind that "Jesus is as close as your heart."

God never forgets His promises. We often do. I forget important spiritual principles as easily as a little task that sends me scurrying, empty-headed, to the next room. Jesus emphasized one of them when He said, "In the world you will have tribulation" (John 16:33). In this world you will have significant earthquakes.

But even that reminder is tied to a marvelous promise by the God who always remembers.

100 Percent Chance of Rain

I was a camp director for years. A favorite project during that season of my life was to involve our campers with an exciting camp theme. We'd have skits and songs and elaborate decorations.

One summer we decided to be *Noah's Navy*. The camp theme and the title of our musical was "100 Percent Chance of Rain." We placed rainbow banners everywhere and staff members dressed in slickers. Every cabin was named after an animal. There was even a gangplank at the chapel and we entered two by two.

I was proud of our efforts to keep everything rolling along the lines of our topic. We sang "Rise and Shine" till we were blue in the face. Over the public address system at any given moment,

I would yell to everyone all over the grounds in my most bellowing voice, *"What's the weather report?"*

From every nook and cranny, every bush or hiking trail would come the answer at the top of healthy nine- and ten-year-old lungs: *"One hundred percent chance of rain!"*

The Truth and Nothing But the Truth

Since then I have learned it over and over in my life, and I would like to warn you of this: It's true. It's a Bible promise. "In the world you *will* have tribulation." Count on it. Jesus said it. He knew the truth because He was the Truth.

Get ready. At some point, if not now, troubles will come. But don't despair. There's more.

"Cheer up!" Jesus said, also in John 16:33, "for I have overcome the world" (TLB). So, if you're having troubles in this world, remember that the God who keeps His promises has you — and the world — in the palm of His hand.

I Promise!

How does that make you feel? That's what we've got going for us. It's 2 Corinthians 1:20: "For all the promises of God in Him are Yes, and in Him Amen, to the glory of God through us."

No matter the size of the quake, no matter how torrential the downpour, God has made a promise. He will gang up on the world and take your side.

Hear the words of Ruth Harms Calkin:

> *Oh, dear God!*
> I've made a profound
> And glorious discovery:
> When the painful circumstances
> Of my listless life
> Shout a fanatic No!
> Jesus Christ, the Victorious One
> Shouts an emphatic Yes![1]

Wouldn't it be wonderful if we could echo back a promise to God? If, from hearts overflowing with love and gratitude, we could hear His voice and in obedience to anything He asks, answer a resounding Yes! Lord, Yes!

Just Say—YES!

Nationally there is an anti-drug campaign. Its slogan is "Just Say No." Sometimes I fear that too many women are learning to just say no to God's ways and ending up empty. How encouraging to find those who refuse to say an automatic "No" to God.

As Dr. E. Stanley Jones says, "Jesus is the Divine Yes. . . . Surrender to His will and you will be saying Yes to His Yes. The whole universe is behind it. You will walk the earth a conqueror, afraid of nothing."[2]

My husband and I were weary to the bone one evening when we arrived home from a week of traveling and ministering. We probably should have gone to bed for much-needed rest, but instead we began to deal with some responsibilities on the homefront and before long we were exchanging some pretty harsh words. I accused David of ignoring my wonderful wisdom in the matters at hand.

Then I used my favorite technique for dealing with problems: the silent treatment. I felt justified. After all, I was right. No doubt about that!

But the Lord was speaking to me deep in my heart: "Daisy, even though you think your husband is wrong, you know what your attitude must be."

Yes, Lord.

"Even though he didn't pay attention to what you were saying and hurt your feelings, you know what your response must be."

Yes, Lord.

Does it take any less grace after forty-one years? *No!* I have to draw again and again on God's power and remember that His strength shows up most clearly in weak people. Apologizing is hard to do, but I decided to say, "Yes, Lord." I think David was surprised when I said I was sorry and dropped the silent treatment. His heart softened too.

All over there are women standing up to allow God to prove that He remembers His promises as they receive strength and courage to say Yes to His will.

I met Mary in North Carolina, a godly working grandmother who has custody of two young grandsons (what a challenge!). Mary is saying Yes.

Last week I talked to Susan in Texas. She is recovering from the guilt of her father's suicide; not giving up. Susan is instead saying Yes, Lord.

Joyce, from Oklahoma, returning to a difficult missionary assignment overseas, is saying Yes, Lord!

Then there's Kay, in Southern California, struggling through a crisis in her husband's life, saying Yes, Lord!

God Kept His Promise

Those women are living one of my favorite Bible promises, which is found in Luke 1:45: "Happy is the woman who believes in God, for his promises to her come true" (PHILLIPS).

What do you think Mrs. Noah had in mind when she married a man that the book of Genesis describes as righteous and faithful? Maybe she thought he'd be a quiet little missionary and their three sons would grow up and get good wives and she'd be knitting booties for her grandchildren by the fireplace someday.

She probably never envisioned the rain and the mud and, worst of all—can you imagine the smell that must have permeated that ark? Whew!

Yet I believe Noah and his wife knew something wonderful and liberating about the promises of God. They knew He doesn't say, "You'll be dry and warm" or "You'll never have a migraine headache." He doesn't even promise that our babies won't die in our arms or that our husbands will remain faithful to us. His promises are bigger than that. He promises He will be faithful for a thousand generations, to be constantly present in times of trouble.

What's the weather forecast? *One hundred percent chance of rain.* Listen, that's reality. But, before I forget . . . let me remind you . . . if you're ever soaking in the tub and the earth starts rumbling, make sure Psalm 46 is hidden in your heart. God's Divine Love Gift to you and me:

He promises refuge.
He promises His strength when you have none.
He promises to be there in your darkest tribulation.

To that, all I can say is . . . "Yes!"

Memo to myself:
    —Practice saying Yes—especially to my family
    —Check out the supplies for earthquake preparedness

Prayer:
    Lord, You are the only One who can really make promises that are guaranteed. Today, may I practice Your promises as well as Your presence. Amen.

Before I forget—I'll do it today:
    What did you do to get through the last "big one" in your life? Do you know someone who might be feeling shattered today? What can you do to help?
    Think of two areas in which you need to say Yes, Lord. Can you talk to God about them and today, lay them down?

Part Three

— ❀ —

*W*hat
We
Must
Forget...
And
Remember

Chapter 7

*F*orget Past Achievements, Failures, and You-Know-Who

Set a guard, O LORD, over my mouth;
Keep watch over the door of my lips.
(Ps. 141:3)

*W*e're told that as the years slip by, some of our faculties slip out. I read recently that we lose one hundred thousand brain cells daily!

Do you relate to that at all? I know that sounds like bad news. But it isn't, entirely. According to God's Word, some things we should be happy to forget if we want to move on successfully in life.

For instance, *forget past achievements.* Chuck Swindoll says, "Don't read your own clippings." Remembering and basking in accomplishments of yesterday will puff up a person.

One bumper sticker read: Don't let your pride get inflated — you may have to swallow it someday! There are other things besides past feats that are better forgotten as well; *past failures,* for instance. And, just as importantly, *the failures of others.* Let's talk about how to make sure past achievements, past failures, and the failures of others don't become unforgettable stumbling blocks instead of time-treasured memorial stones.

Forget Past Achievements

It happens to me frequently. It happened again. I was flipping through my notes, munching on a delicious bite of strawberry shortcake at the banquet where I was about to speak when the chairman leaned over from her seat at the head table to whisper in my ear.

"Daisy," she said, as if our conversation was top secret, "how would you like to be introduced?" I was tempted to tell her how I'd *really* like to be described in front of that group of women. How often I have sat and admired a speaker who was presented as one who had traveled the globe, graduated with honors from esteemed universities, or dined with celebrities.

I smiled at the thought of it and she must have wondered what I was thinking. How would I like to be introduced? "Ladies! Your attention, please! Our renowned speaker, Doctor Daisy, has a Ph.D. in ... everything. She has written twenty-five — make it thirty — best-selling books. Her husband is the President of the World, and her children are beauty contest winners, heads of state, and Olympic gold medal recipients."

After that I thought for a moment about listing some of the small exploits that stood out as significant accomplishments for a woman who is packed full of ordinariness. But none of them seemed to qualify me at the moment.

So I said, "Well, I'm a wife and mother. A housekeeper. No, wait a minute. I'm a *homemaker* (don't you think that gives it a little more dignity?) ... a Domestic Engineer."

"Hmmm," she said. "Shall I introduce you now? Or shall I let them go on having a good time?"

Peacock Feathers

Isn't it funny how we go to great lengths to make our achievements sound worthwhile? I overheard one mother mentioning that she had seen her daughter's résumé. She giggled at the word *nanny*.

"My daughter was a babysitter," she said, "but 'nanny' sounded more sophisticated!"

Here's an important proverb someone passed along:

> It doesn't pay to get "stuck up";
>   Remember
> The peacock of today may be a
>   feather duster tomorrow.

Unfortunately, the world around us measures our worth and effectiveness by our achievements. Some people are over- qualified-super-achievers and want to make sure the rest of the world appreciates it.

Forget-Me-Nots

A friend brought this example home to me. A vivacious, godly, devoted young wife had just engineered the all-time world-champion Christmas party for her husband's office staff. In contemplating how she was really going to pull off this event, she confided over the telephone that she was already dreaming up ways to make sure everyone at the party would realize how much work she had gone to.

She recruited some of the office women as hostesses. However, what she really had in mind was for them to line up and watch her carry in large, elegant trays of food. The extravagant party games were designed to accentuate elaborate door prizes my friend prepared. She was sure everyone would "ooh" and "aah" over her fine efforts. We did giggle when we both saw the vanity of it all!

That's when it hit me: It's built right into the incredible, sometimes unbeatable pride factor in our lives, isn't it? That urge we have to appear as something more than we are. Sure, we're willing to serve, willing to do for others — we just don't want them to forget!

New Price Tags

The apostle Paul described this innate human tendency when he told the church at Philippi, with its struggling class differences, that some things had to be put into perspective.

"If anyone else thinks he may have confidence in the flesh, I more so: circumcised on the eighth day, of the stock of Israel, of the tribe of Benjamin, a Hebrew of the Hebrews; concerning the law, a Pharisee; concerning zeal, persecuting the church; concerning righteousness which is the law, blameless" (Phil. 3:4-6).

Among peers his accomplishments were a source of pride. But Paul had come to the place where he saw that everything the world counted as a qualification was worthless compared with the priceless gain of knowing Christ.

My husband says that as the years go by most people seem to "switch price tags." Things that used to be valuable lose some of their importance as others become more precious. Have you seen this happen? This proves that we can choose where we place value. Paul certainly did. "I also count all things loss for the excellence of the knowledge of Christ Jesus my Lord" (Phil. 3:8).

Why is it so easy to remember our achievements? And why is it a special act of faith and commitment to forget them?

My husband once wrote:

> Powerful words: helpless, worthless, priceless. Does it appear degrading to declare my achievements as worthless? After all, those achievements represent valuable years of hard work and sacrifice, and the product of this labor has kept our family comfortable and secure.
>
> This is true for most, I guess. But still we know we are helpless to save ourselves, and as God's grace glows in its pricelessness, our own achievements pale into insignificance.
>
> I remember when I started my career, my first job. I thought, I will do *whatever it takes* to succeed. After all, that's the work ethic that has built America! Paul implies that when we realize new life in Christ for the dynamic experience it is, we shift our focus. We can choose to switch off the success mode, and switch on the desire to be faithful.
>
> *Lord, help me today to take my eyes off the worthless things and place them on the priceless Redeemer. Change my desires to impress and possess to desires for the fulfillment of Your purposes in my life today. Amen.*

Just Forget It!

When tempted to elevate past achievements above feather-duster status, I remember the lines of an old poem:

Forget each kindness that you do as soon as you have done it.
Forget the praise that falls to you the moment you have won it.
Forget the slander that you hear before you can repeat it.
Forget each slight, each spite, each sneer, whenever you may meet it.
Remember every promise made and keep it to the letter.
Remember those who lend you aid and be a grateful debtor.
Remember all the happiness that comes your way in living.
Forget each worry and distress, be hopeful and forgiving.
Remember good, remember truth, remember heaven is above you.
And you will find, through age and youth, that many will love you.

A well-known pastor was examining Scripture and wondering why God dealt with the sin of pride so harshly. He inquired of an older brother in the ministry and the answer came. "Well, son, it's plain to see. Every other sin a man commits, he commits out of his need. But the sin of pride indicates that he has no need. And God will not forgive sin until we acknowledge our need — pride blinds us to our need."

Forget Past Failures

I just turned sixty. Coming home from a seminar where the topic was "Get Up and Grow," I stopped to receive a handful of cards and letters from our mailman. In great anticipation of all the adulation and hoopla my friends would be making over this milestone I barely made it inside my front door before I dropped my bags and began happily tearing open the envelopes.

After reading two or three cards filled with sentiment and fun, I stared at one that momentarily stunned me. (The seminar ladies would have said it "stunted my growth" — get it?) Even though I hadn't been quite prepared for the message, I had to admit there was a great lesson behind the words on that greeting card.

Happy Birthday?

On the cover was a drooping, wilted daisy. I've always thought of the daisy as sort of my personal coat-of-arms. But not this one! It had weepy leaves, a warped stem, and loose petals scattered on the ground.

I hate to admit it, but maybe I am getting a bit droopy, I thought as I pondered the words on the front of the card.

The text said something about how depressing it is to have a birthday and that getting older is no picnic and gray hair is no fun and life doesn't go the way you planned it and on and on. . . .

The inside simply exclaimed in bold, black print:

"Oh grow up!"

It wasn't what I expected for a birthday greeting, but it was and is a good word of advice. My friend knew I'd appreciate the meaning and how it tied in with my messages encouraging women to "Get Up and Grow!"

Wilted or Willing?

Too many times past failures leave me feeling wilted. Hanging on to the regrets from yesterday's mistakes can only make me droop. I think this is what the Word of God has to say about forgetting all the stuff that is behind us: "Grow up!" If you don't want to drop any more precious petals of opportunity in life, let go of all you have not realized and move on into the nourishing soil of a new day.

For me this happens when I realize that all my dreams probably won't come true. Even armed with the world's best diet and my exercise bike, I'll probably never be svelte. I'll probably never be rich and famous. (Someone said that a more realistic TV show would be entitled, "Lifestyles of the Poor and Obscure"!) And, worse than anything else, I will probably never experience a time in my life when I've pleased everyone or felt liked and appreciated by 100 percent of my acquaintances and loved ones.

Once, after speaking at a convention, I received a negative, critical, unsigned letter. Like most people, even if I get thousands of pats on the back, dozens of letters of encouragement, scores of affirming phone calls, and maybe even flowers, I can still be devastated by one negative comment.

After reading the letter, I phoned a friend in tears. "What should I do?" I felt like quitting. But after prayer and the encouragement of a Christian sister, I realized what I must do. I must give up. Let go. Not of my ministry, but of my reputation.

As Paul said of Jesus in Philippians 2, we are to have the attitude of Jesus Christ, who made Himself of no reputation. When I let go, I feel the hope of tomorrow. I feel the protection of a God who controls my future.

Paul said it best. "One thing I do, forgetting those things which are behind and reaching forward to those things which are ahead,

I press toward the goal for the prize of the upward call of God in Christ Jesus" (Phil. 3:13-14).

Happy New Year!

Author Chuck Swindoll points out:

> There is not a single saint who sits in a church anywhere who does not have a few things he or she is ashamed of. The one who thinks otherwise is worse than all the rest of us combined. We were all taken from the same dunghill; we all fight the filth of the flesh regardless of how loudly we sing, how pious we look or how sweetly we say "hello."
>
> When God forgives, He forgets. He is not only pleased but thrilled to use any vessel — just as long as it is clean today. It may be cracked or chipped, it may be worn, or it may have never been used before. You can count on this — the past ended one second ago. As we start a new year you can be clean, filled with His Spirit and used in many different ways for His honor. God's glorious grace says: "Draw the anchor, trim the sails, man the rudder, look ahead . . . a strong gale is coming!"

Happy New You!

Doesn't that give you hope? It does me. Are you thinking right now about some of that old baggage you thought you'd have to drag around forever? Did you think those failed attempts to please others, get straight A's, land that perfect job, or have a flawless family meant you could never get up and start again?

Did you imagine that no one has ever sunk to the depths of sin you have? Listen to what Jeremiah, who is known as the Weeping Prophet, said: "Remember my affliction and roaming, / The wormwood and the gall. / My soul still remembers / And sinks within me" (Lam. 3:19-20).

That's exactly what happens when we carry with us the baggage of yesterday. All of our failures. All of our ineffectiveness. All of the times we did not do as we know we perhaps ought to have done. All of our lethargy. Our ho-humness. We remember all of that and it only serves to defeat and to discourage.

Then the prophet speaks this wonderful word, "This I recall to my mind, / Therefore I have hope. / Through the LORD's mercies we are not consumed, / Because His compassions fail not. / They are new every morning; / Great is Your faithfulness" (Lam. 3:21-23).

Don't forget: God's grace is all about forgetting past failures. With God, every day is New Year's Day. Every day is New You Day!

"Oh grow up!" His Spirit lovingly prods. "Forget past failures and press on."

Forget the Failures of Others

My husband was born on Thanksgiving Day. And it was on a Thanksgiving Day when he was nineteen years old that he surrendered his heart and life to the Lord Jesus.

David loves to tell the story about how, after a simple gospel message, the likes of which he had heard countless times in his life, my own grandmother came and tapped him on the shoulder and said, "Isn't today the day, David?"

And as he went forward, my dear Grandma Cowan walked up to the little altar there in the front of the Salvation Army chapel in Mount Vernon, New York, and knelt beside him.

It was also Thanksgiving time when, as a teenager, David learned a painful lesson, one he is now grateful for because it made him a person who can forget the failures of others.

"I was in serious trouble," David remembers. "Somehow, after the policeman left our home, my father saw past the hurt and embarrassment and assured me of his forgiveness."

Even though David's mistake was very serious, when Dad Hepburn saw true remorse, he promised never to bring up the happenings of that day again.

"And you know," David muses with a tear in the corner of his eye, "Dad kept his promise. During that teachable, tender moment in my life, Dad chose to put that experience away 'as far as the east is from the west.' And he never mentioned it again. I felt loved, not exasperated. My wise father taught me how to be a forgiving father."

Remember to Forget

Last spring I was traveling in the highlands of Scotland. I've often been curious about my Scottish heritage. As a young girl, I was often moved as Grandpa Cowan, with his heavy Scottish brogue, would tell stories of the old country.

Grandpa had given his life to the Lord when he was only seventeen. Even after a farm equipment accident left one leg permanently lame, Grandpa served his God fervently as an officer of the Salvation Army until he was seventy-seven years old. I remember how thrilled I was when he gave me fifty cents for learning the Lord's Prayer and the afternoon he spent teaching me how to do a kind of highland fling until I made believe I really had seen the blue bells of Scotland and heard the drone of bagpipes.

So when the tour bus driver pulled over to the Lakeside Cafe by Loch Lomond, over tea and scones I inquired if this was in fact the sight of the Colquhoun clan. He assured me it was and seemed delighted to have an audience for his version of the great feud that plagued the clan.

Apparently there were Colquhoun clanners on the islands as well as on the mainland. They worked on the vast estate of the landowner, but the two sets of clanners were at odds. When they had to contact each other in town they were quick to realize their differences.

I was anxious to get to the bottom of the problem and fix it! After all, they were my ancestors, so I asked, "What was the reason for the actual feud? I mean, what was the basic argument?"

The tour guide thought for a minute and rubbed his chin. "You know," he said with a perplexed look, "that's the silly thing. They fought for all that time over who was right and who was wrong. But, lassie, no one could really remember what started it all!"

Practically speaking, what a release there is in being able to forget and not drag old baggage with us into the freedom we can enjoy. Just this week I was faced again with the choices we have. It was when an old friend reminded me of something very hurtful that happened several years ago.

Someone I had trusted had let me down. It wasn't easy, but I truly forgave that person. Now, after all this time, when my friend brought it up and said, "Remember when ... ?" I knew I needed to make another choice. I answered simply with a smile, "No, I distinctly remember forgetting that!" And I did.

Karen Mains gives wise exhortation in *The Key to an Open Heart*.

1. I forgive people for all the things they haven't done—
    -for no phone calls when I was absent or in great need of spirit.
    -for those who have withheld love when I desperately needed love extended.
    -for no one caring for me as a person, but for everyone only wanting from me the things I can do for them.

2. I forgive people for the things that have been said—
    -the words, words, words, that harm me more than sticks and stones and sometimes damage me in deeper, more lasting ways.
    -words traveling through third parties.
    -criticism, jealousy, gossip, sugar-coated in devious love, a truly bitter pill.
    -pious phrases telling me how to improve myself when I thought I was really making progress in that area.

3. I forgive those in our church body who have been inadequate friends—
    -those who have rejected my efforts to reach out.
    -those who refuse to forgive me for things I have done.
    -those who don't know how to be a friend unless I do the calling, seeking out, initiating.

    We forgive, Father; be pleased to work the release of forgiveness in our hearts.[1]

Short Accounts

What Mrs. Mains and that dear woman illustrate is an important concept that I learned best from my friend Juanita when she went through the incredible grief of losing her best friend, her confidant, her lover — her husband, through sudden death.

"Daisy, I had no idea there was this much pain involved. I am fifty-three years old and I can't imagine spending the rest of my life without my best friend. I just feel like saying, 'Lord, I want Reg back.' I want him to walk in the door. I don't care if he's going to be sick the rest of his life. I just want him to be here with me."

We sobbed together over the phone. I could hear Juanita's searing pain as she told me about the sudden shock. The day before was Thanksgiving Day and Juanita and her two grown children had celebrated in the hospital room. Reg cheered during football games and prayed with his grateful little family, thanking God for their many blessings.

The greatest blessing was the doctors' assurance that Reg would be okay. The treatments were working. One more round and they were sure of victory. So, when Juanita received a phone call the next morning telling her that her beloved Reggie was slipping fast, she was horrified.

Dressing quickly, she made it to the hospital in record time. She glanced at the huge, round clock hanging above the wall at the nurses' station. Six-thirty. "Please, God, don't take him. Please, let me see him again."

Forty-five minutes later, while Juanita clung to his hand, Reg breathed his last breath.

"Juanita, . . ." my mind was racing. I wanted to reach across those thousands of miles between us and comfort my precious friend. "Juanita, does it help at all to know that Reg is so much better off — he is with Jesus?"

"No—because I'm so much worse off!" She answered without hesitation. "We were going to grow old together, retire together. We even had tickets for a special trip. It wasn't supposed to be like this."

My attempts at condolence seemed so feeble. I knew I couldn't understand or even imagine her pain that was, at this moment, like a huge, fresh, gaping wound.

"Juanita, dear, listen. Psalm 91 says that God will give His angels charge and they will watch over you."

"I don't want angels. I want Reg."

There was silence for a time, except for whimpering that sounded like a wounded child. I prayed in silence, asking God to give some comforting thought to this woman who had often been a comfort and inspiration to me.

Juanita is a strong, mature Christian. She had faced some hard challenges in her life, but none like this. I was grateful for the opportunity to grieve with this dear friend and asked God to help me carry some of her pain.

Just as my thoughts and prayers seemed to be giving way to words, Juanita surprised me.

"There is one thing that really brings me a lot of comfort," she said.

I waited quietly to hear the encouragement God had given her.

"It's the fact that Reg and I were forgiven up-to-date. We kept short accounts. It's comforting to know that I have no regrets."

Tears brimmed over and spilled onto the mouthpiece of my telephone. My breath caught as I tried to respond. I couldn't seem to say anything. I was thinking of my own life and the soul-piercing challenge of Juanita's words. Would I have regrets? Are my accounts short with those who mean the most to me?

Juanita broke into my thoughts, "I think that's why I could stand there this morning while the doctors were baffled and say, 'I've staked my life on the promises of God . . . and they're all true.' I wasn't caught up in regrets and bitterness and it made it easier to tell those doctors that none of us knows what's ahead, but we know that God is faithful. I think it helped them to hear that."

That's when I knew Juanita would be fine. She was already thinking of the welfare of others.

It's just past Christmas as I'm writing this. I received a beautiful Christmas card from Juanita and her family. Her hand-written note said that Reg had picked out the cards on Thanksgiving Day. The text, which now seems prophetic, reads:

> Despite uncertain days,
> I am rapturous — quite!
> Regularly enjoined by angels —
> singing in the night.
>
> Further,
> I hear what angels herald;
> Divine decree —
> The sweet Infant cry
> of Creation — calling me.[2]

Reg must have heard the angels calling. Juanita did, too, though she didn't realize it. They'd been calling all along for her to live up-to-date in forgiveness. To keep accounts short. To say when old hurts and the failures of others pop into mind, "I distinctly remember forgetting that."

Forget past achievements. Forget past failures. Forget the

failures of others. If I'm really losing one hundred thousand brain cells a day, I hope they're the ones holding the data about my successes and failures. And the only thing I want to remember about other people's mistakes is that I remembered to forget them.

Memo to myself
— List a dozen or so failures I have experienced . . . then tear up the list. Do the same with a few achievements
— Sing all the verses of "Great Is Thy Faithfulness"

Prayer:
Help me to remember, Lord, to forget!

Before I forget—I'll do it today:
Do you need to shift price tags on some values today? Choose one and do it. Act on your decision, somehow, today.
What mistakes—yours or others'—are stunting your growth? Write them down, tear them up, and ask God to help you forget them.

Chapter 8

Remember: Marshmallows First

But seek first the kingdom of God and His righteousness,
and all these things shall be added to you.
(Matt. 6:33)

*T*he little pint jar always arouses curiosity. I carry it with me and people think I'm a junk-food junkie. Actually, that clear glass container is a visual aid.

It holds two cups of M&M's candies and a dozen marshmallows. I can do this visual aid with rice, but the M&M's remind me of Mary and Martha.

You see, the jar is supposed to be my day. The M&M's represent all kinds of small elements of living . . . the daily routines . . . you know, all the stuff that's going to fill up the jar too quickly.

The marshmallows represent the mandates of the Word of God. They are the bigger, more important elements. Several spiritual marshmallows, like prayer, Bible reading, and serving others, must be included in the dailiness of life.

Yet it's so easy to forget them. Especially if you do what I do all too often—get the jar filled up with M&M's first so the marshmallows don't fit.

However, I have found that if the marshmallows go in first, everything fits. Try it yourself. You can see that putting first things first works out best. That's exactly what the Bible teaches: "Seek first the kingdom of God."

Please Don't Forget

What should be our first concern, what is of ultimate worth to our Lord and Savior right this minute is our having a vitally alive and personal communication going with Him now and all the time.

There's really only one thing worth being concerned about and between Mary and Martha, only the former discovered it. Mary found out about marshmallows and M&M's (sort of). She put the big things in first so everything else would fit.

Evelyn Minshull wrote a beautiful article that captures the essence of the M&M story. It is appropriately entitled "Priorities."

> Even when we were children, Mary wasted time.
>
> If Mother said to gather herbs, I gathered herbs. *Mary* would pause to sniff a lily, stroke its petals, follow a sparrow's spiraling across the sky. . . .
>
> When we were fully grown *my* housekeeping was flawless, Mary's flawed by bits of dust, neglected; a jug, unwashed; a rug, unshaken.
>
> The day the Master came, when there were other guests, so much to do (the oil to fetch, fruits to arrange, small, spicy cakes to shape, the linen to be spread—so *much* to do my mind was reeling with it) and Mary, bright-eyed and

smiling like a child, curled up to listen at the Master's feet. It angered me.

And so — the flour smear still on my skirt, my finger smarting from a cut, my forearm reddened by a spatter of hot oil — I told the Master, expecting at least, perhaps, His hand upon my shoulder.... But He was not supportive (though still kind, of course, that loving sorrow in His eyes).

"Martha," he murmured, "Martha . . . you are careful and troubled about many things, but one thing is needful, and Mary has chosen that good thing...."

All of my life, I'd worshiped work. I had a house whose neatness was the envy of the village, some recipes the other women praised and calloused hands and knees.

But *Mary* had a million memories of captured sunlight . . . and she had won the Master's praise, not I.

I wondered . . . could it be I — not Mary — who all those years had wasted so much time?[1]

The Misty Flats

Time.

More than thirty years had passed. I had forgotten. That was when I first read a verse quoted in a book by Isobel Kuhns. The woman and her choice of words found a home in my soul, teaching me softly about priorities:

> To every man there openeth
> A way, and ways, and a way.
> And the high soul climbs the high way,
> And the low soul gropes the low.
> *And in between on the misty flats*

The rest drift to and fro.
But to every man there openeth
A high way and a low —
And every man decideth the way his soul shall go.[2]

My Mentor

"Daisy, do you realize who this woman is?"

It was last year at the Great Smokey Mountains women's retreat. Late at night. Way up in the beautiful wooded hills in a conference center where the leaders were clad in housecoats and slippers, conferring about hairdos and weight loss and how good everyone looked since the last time we were together.

It was my good friend Bea who said, "Daisy, I'll bet you can never guess in a million years who Kathy Ruleson is."

Well, I knew she was the guest missionary speaker and she was leading the devotional sessions. And I knew she and her husband had served the Lord in Thailand for many years. But it took my breath away when Bea said, "Kathy is the daughter of Isobel Kuhn."

"Oh my!" I thought. "Imagine that — Isobel Kuhn's very own daughter — and I'm meeting her right here!"

As a young, impressionable woman thirty years ago, I had been introduced to her mother's books. Oh, what an impact they had on my life! I had devoured, with wonder, the four volumes that told of Isobel's life and ministry to the Lisu Indians in Thailand.

For Isobel Kuhn, there was "a way, and a way" and her high soul climbed the high way of service. Though it was a way of obscurity without fame or fortune, she left the misty flats to follow her Savior. I remembered reading of her family and of the daughter I was now meeting face to face.

Out of the Fog

Amazingly, I felt like the young woman I once was. The strong desire to follow in the footsteps of that wonderful mentor I never knew — except on typeset page — came flooding back.

As soon as I returned to San Francisco from the Smokey Mountains, I reread all four of Mrs. Kuhn's books. *By Searching: My Journey Through Doubt Into Faith* caused me to renew again my commitment to stay out of the mist and choose not to grope along the low ways.

You and I do have choices. Mary chose. Martha also chose. Some climb the high way; some grope the low. Many others drift about on misty flats in kind of the gray area — the fogginess.

I have to tell you, I am really terrified of fog. In fog, you can't see what's in front or behind. Fog is the most treacherous freeway condition. Spiritual fog is also perilous. Those who linger in fog wallow around in mediocrity. By not choosing they choose. By not choosing, they automatically travel the low way.

Paul said we should choose the high way: "Set your mind on things above" (Col. 3:2). Get out of the fog. So many drift to and fro on the misty flats. But don't you do it. You climb the highway of holiness. Aim for something loftier, something crystal clear.

This has been a year of renewal for me. Since the Smokey Mountain experience, I have thought, *How good of God to have brought this woman and this quote back into my life, knowing what it would mean to me*. It was a very important time for me to consider my calendar and ways I needed to make some specific choices on how I would invest my energy and time in days ahead.

I want to be increasingly careful, especially since the years seem to be flying by, that I spend my energies in endeavors that matter for eternity. While I was sharing with a group of seminary student wives, one burdened young mother asked me pointed questions about balancing her busy life. She was working full time, caring for two small children, keeping a home, and serving in her church.

She was exhausted and challenged me to give her some answers. When I spoke to her, I was speaking to myself. "Keep eternity's values in view." That concept has been renewing for me. When I feel overwhelmed and underappreciated, I stop, and, thinking of the misty flats, ask myself three questions:

1. How can I simplify?

2. In this situation, what will endure throughout eternity?

3. Whom am I striving to please? Myself? Others? Jesus?

I suggested to that young wife that she go through her house and subtract, rather than add, pictures on the walls, bric-a-brac, or knickknacks. Making home visually simpler and serene can help us focus on what's important and create a peaceful atmosphere.

After sharing that message with the women, I was inspired myself and on the ride home from the airport, I visualized how I could go through some boxes and reduce the clutter in my own home.

As a young woman I knew Isobel Kuhn as a wonderful role model through her books. Now, these many years later, I have realized the privilege of becoming a role model for my own daughter and occasionally for other young women. Isobel's daughter Kathy told me wonderful stories of the life and death of her dear mother, who went to heaven when she was only fifty-five years old.

Kathy became a treasure to me. She reminded me of books, life-altering commitments, of the beauty of simplicity and the importance of keeping eternal values always in view, of her mother . . . of the misty flats.

Through her, God whispered to me again, "Daisy, don't forget to put first things first."

Memo to myself:
— Fill a jar with marshmallows and M&M's and put it on my kitchen shelf as a reminder
— Check out a missionary biography from the church library . . . find time to read it

Prayer:
So many choices challenge me today. Teach me, Lord, to choose the highest and best—to be able to recognize You beckoning me out of the misty flats. Amen.

Before I forget—I'll do it today:
What "high way" beckons you today? What steps can you take forward on it?
How can you create a memorial stone of your mentor for a young woman you know?

Chapter 9

A Wreath on the Chimney!

During those celebration days each year you must explain to your children why you are celebrating—it is a celebration of what the Lord did for you when you left Egypt.
(Exod. 13:8 TLB)

*I*t was a hot, humid, misty day as my husband and I set out with our little girl to visit the leper colony in the hills of Puerto Rico. I was feeling terrible. Some type of cold or virus was sapping my strength, and I remember the self-pity that had me thinking: *I can't handle one more event to celebrate Christmas!*

Have you ever felt like that? You know: Others have everything going for them. It's easy for them to have a party. But what have you and I got to celebrate? We have *real* problems. Right?

I'm so glad you understand!

Streams of sweat ran down under the collar of my blue Salvation Army uniform while David whistled "Jingle Bells" and steered our rickety automobile up through the palm trees along a winding dirt road. Even little Lois seemed to catch the spirit of the holidays as she played with a bright ribbon on one of the packages I had painstakingly wrapped.

Ignoring my family's perky mood, I managed to grumble the entire length of the journey, feeling very ill and justified in my demeanor. When we finally arrived and located the meeting hall, I began to set up a flannel-graph story board and sheet music for Christmas carols.

In my very best Spanish (which wasn't great), I relayed the Christmas story and led singing in an effort to minister to the thirty-three residents who all shared the misfortune of living out their days with the devastating disease of leprosy. Outwardly, I muddled through my mission in an effort to appear appropriately joyful for the season. But, on the inside, I was still finding things to complain about.

The Man With No Fingers

Why did I have to give up my afternoon to swelter on a hilltop? Didn't I have enough work to do already? My own Christmas gifts weren't wrapped yet. The house had to be decorated. And besides all of that, why did we have to be here in this unbearable heat while our friends and family back in the States were probably building snowmen and baking Christmas cookies?

Of course, my heart went out to these people. But feeling sick in body and terribly sorry for myself in spirit, I brought our simple service to a quick close, thankful that the Spirit of God is not bound by our infirmities or attitudes.

Now it was time for the distribution of the gifts. I took a box that contained packages of toiletry items, candy, and small, practical objects. One by one, grateful individuals came forward, smiling from ear to ear as they each received something. It was evident that this tiny gesture meant so much to them.

To my great dismay I handed a small bag of candy to a man who had no fingers. He looked at the bag with the curly red ribbon tied in a knot around the top. I looked at his hands and at the stubs where his fingers used to be. My gaze dropped to the floor as my cheeks burned red hot with humiliation and . . . something else.

At first I wasn't sure what it was. Then I knew. It was shame. I had been complaining about the heat. About the long journey. About giving up my time. I guess you could say I was whimpering about having no gloves until I met someone who had no fingers. . . .

Our eyes met for a moment. My heart sank as I awkwardly unwrapped the candy for that dear one. With my own healthy fingers I brushed away the tear on my cheek and moved toward the next person.

When it was time for us to leave we were called to attention as the very same man with no fingers stood and with great enthusiasm thanked us for the wonderful celebration we had brought to their secluded colony. He went on and on.

His joy embarrassed me. And I prayed,

> Dear Lord Jesus,
> Forgive me.
> My dull spirit of
> celebration
> needs polishing.
> Forgive and
> Shine through me —
> in spite of myself

and the times
I'm whole
on the outside
but missing something
important
on the inside.
Remind me often
that to celebrate
with joy
I don't need
comfort
   or
good health
   or
cool weather
   or even
all my parts.
All I need to celebrate
is You.
Amen.

Celebration Is Identification

I've learned that the celebration of my life is my mark of identification. In Exodus 13:16 we read, "This celebration shall identify you as God's people, just as much as if his brand of ownership were placed upon your foreheads" (TLB).

Moses told the Israelites to celebrate what God had done in Egypt when the death angel had passed over them. Every year during the Passover celebration they would be able to tell their children about God's great miracles.

Celebrations require preparation. I guess I can't remember a time when my children actually asked me why we were celebrating. But they have asked, "Mom, why are you vacuuming and it's not even Saturday morning?" or "Why did you put fresh flowers on the kitchen table? Is company coming over?" or "Why do we go to church every Sunday?" The answer to all of these questions is, "To celebrate, of course!" We remember and we celebrate the powerful things God has done to bring us through this far! And in that celebration we identify with the One who has given so much for us.

A Celebration of Memories

Reminiscence automatically happens during celebrations. On your anniversary, did you and your spouse ever spend time trying to remember where you spent your last anniversary? Or the first? At a class reunion, didn't you sit around with friends and discuss the "good old days"? (Someone said that if you're longing for the good old days . . . just turn off the air conditioning!)

Pastor Duane L. Storey says that a "celebration of memories stirs up within us appreciation, wonder and love."[1] God knew the connection between celebrating and remembering. That's why He placed a strong emphasis on taking time to plan and schedule celebrations that are meaningful and that move us out of the mundane.

When Jesus said, "Do this in remembrance of Me" (Luke 22:19), He initiated a "celebration of memories." Now every time believers partake of the bread and wine in a Communion service, we are filled with thanksgiving and joy because we remember what God did for us through His Son on the cross at Calvary.

As I write this we are in that significant time of year for remembering the Last Supper. It's just a few days before Easter.

Several special friends have made a trip to the Holy Land this spring, and as I listen to their reports about walking the streets of Jerusalem and going into the room where this Supper could have taken place, I try to picture myself in that room seated at the table.

"Do this in remembrance of Me," I can hear Jesus say as He breaks the bread and pours the wine (Luke 22:19). I think of the tokens at our modern communion table, tokens in the application of the grace of God through the sacrifice of Jesus that remind me of His goodness.

Author Tim Hansel says that remembering the good times of the past is like "tasting life twice." When we prepare a celebration of memories, we taste again the good things God has done for us.

A Wreath on the Chimney

There are many ways to remember to celebrate. I learned a new one once in Minnesota while stopped at an intersection. The thick white flurries dancing around my car and the crunch of snow and ice under my tires made me grip the wheel with a fair amount of tension. Just then I looked up and saw a wide, green wreath wired to the top of a chimney on the house across the street.

It was well into January, and I figured someone had forgotten to take it down. But the "Happy Holidays!" message was a cheery one, so who would mind? To my surprise, the next month when I was driving through the same area, the wreath was still there. *Happy Valentine's Day* was the new message on the wreath with a big, red ribbon.

In March it became a St. Patrick's Day wreath.

In April the yellow ribbon read: *This is a Happy Easter Wreath!*

Then, in May, believe it or not: *Happy Memorial Day*.

I'll always remember that chimney and the challenge in my heart to remember to celebrate all year long. Is that a reminder you need too?

It's better to remember the good times and practice celebrations of our memories than to rehearse all the bad, disappointing times. It really does take practice, though.

Recently I received a card from a friend that reads something like, "Thanks so much. I'll never forget your kindness, unless a brick hits me in the head, effectively removing my memory and forcing me to spend the rest of my life searching for my identity. . . . In that case, I might not remember, but I'll have some nebulous idea that I had been happy once." Smile.

Remember to celebrate. It's worth it. I'll never forget the man at the leper colony who didn't need fingers to celebrate. Or the wreath on the chimney and the reminder that we don't have to stop celebrating when the holidays are over.

God's Word reminds us that celebrating His deeds is a way of acknowledging His goodness. And so I wake up every morning now and pray, "Lord, is today a good day to hang a wreath on the chimney?"

You could too.

Memo to myself:
  — *Flowers and candles on table tonight*
  — *Balloons?*
  — *Hang a wreath on my chimney*

Prayer:
  Lord, we have so much to celebrate! Let someone notice my wreath and recognize that in our home we are a family celebrating—You! Amen.

Before I forget—I'll do it today:
  What's keeping you from celebrating today? Find something— anything—to cheer about and do so, even if you have a headache. . . .

Chapter 10

A Complete Puzzle

If you want favor with both God and man,
and a reputation for good judgment and common sense,
then trust the Lord completely; don't ever trust yourself.
In everything you do, put God first, and he will direct
you and crown your efforts with success.
(Prov. 3:4-6 TLB)

S he didn't mean it to be funny. But it was okay that everyone chuckled openly at the deep truth behind her words.

"Be-Be-Before . . ." the young woman stammered nervously as she stood during a sharing time at a women's retreat.

Swallowing hard after a brief pause, she finally found courage to continue: "Before I came to know Jesus Christ, my life was like a puzzle with one piece missing."

"But now," she added carefully, "now that I know Christ as my Savior, my life is a . . . a . . . a complete puzzle."

She had said it for all of us profoundly, simply, and truthfully. And most of us could relate.

Completing the Puzzle

Even for those who rest in the saving arms of Jesus, life can be puzzling at times. Whether it's an out-of-balance checking account or a dress pattern that is too much for the fabric you bought or two commitments and a phone call for the same time slot, we often fail to see the picture on the puzzle box top that gives us an idea about where all the fragments fit.

How can I know the Lord's special will for this situation? Should I lead the Sunday school class? homeschool my child? work part-time to supplement our income? or start a neighborhood Bible study group? The hours and minutes of my week are a jigsaw mixture sometimes, with no obvious border — and colors that are hard to sort out.

Sometimes the shape of new circumstances doesn't seem to fit and questions come. Who will care for my children if this puzzling illness is more serious than it appears? The doctors don't seem to have the missing pieces, and I'm not sure where to turn or whom to trust. Why would God allow me to lose my job right now? How could my best friend let me down this way when I needed her more than ever?

A Puzzling Paradox

I have a wonderful friend in Florida who shared with me in a letter the puzzle she was pondering as a growing Christian who wanted to know why God allows some to suffer and some to receive showers of blessing.

Her words were deeply meaningful to me as she voiced some

of my own heart's musings, and I have gone back to read them many times:

> Dear Daisy,
>
> How I appreciated your last letter and the thought from Daniel 3, "God is able to do whatever He wills — but even if He doesn't deliver us — we will serve no other God." We stand in our commitment to Christ — not because it *works*, but because it's *true!*
>
> I remember reading Betty Elliot's book, *A Slow and Certain Light*, at nearly the same time I was reading another author's book. I was astounded at the difference between the two. I said, *"Lord*, could these two women possible serve the *same* God?" Betty has told of having an *entire year's work* on her first linguistic project in a remote tribe being *stolen* as she made her way out of the jungle to marry Jim Elliot. Then the loss of Jim and the other four beautiful, young, committed missionaries and all that went with that tragedy, and its followup with her life in the Auca villages. Then to bring Valerie home for education and marry the second time only to have him soon die a slow, torturous death from cancer. . . .
>
> Meanwhile, the other author, having *every* prayer she *ever* uttered answered exactly on her terms — whether it be a parking place or a matching color blouse, or healing for a common cold or terminal cancer. God seemed to be a "yes man" for one woman, while seemingly nonexistent for the other. Interesting, huh?
>
> Guess I identify better with Betty E. Having lived this long (nearly half a *century*) I've seen too many believers almost hanging on by their fingernails declaring, "Though He slay me, yet will I trust Him," assuming that restoration of Job's kind will only happen in heaven.

I see these very same people carrying on, *exuding great joy in serving Jesus*, functioning normally and caringly and miraculously!   Living for Christ is so paradoxical! I *love* paradoxes. I *live* on them! They are a sign of truth too big for me. . . .

> Much love,
> Sharon

Truth Too Big!

I know that Sharon was not being critical of anyone whose prayers are answered! She was just in awe that God will operate so differently in each life. He does it to bring glory to His name, and we dare not second-guess His working of the creation puzzle.

The last sentence in my friend's letter has been written on my heart since I read it: *Paradoxes are a sign of truth too big for me*. That's why trust has become such an important cornerstone in my own relationship with Christ. As the fearful passenger on a 747 jet must rely on engines and wings and pilots and air pressure and things she knows nothing about (I'm speaking from first-hand, white-knuckle experience) to enjoy the benefits of air travel, so it is with the believer.

Someone has told me that the wings of an airplane are named "Trust" and "Obey" — for there's no other way!

Remembering to trust God will not always spare us from being hurt. But trusting Him habitually for bigger and bigger things will strengthen the walls of our faith until we will have protection from the kind of grievous hurt that can only be felt by those who don't know God and His peace.

No Good Thing

A good example of this happened during my freshman year in college. There was great excitement in the dorm! Carol had landed a date with a BMOC (that's an ancient acronym for Big Man on Campus). She had pressed and set aside her best dress for the occasion.

For a group of girls, seventeen and eighteen, who had been reared in conservative Christian homes and literally raised in church, this college stuff was a real adventure! What a comedy as six of us tripped over each other to help our dorm sister get ready.

We chewed our nails as the appointed hour arrived . . . then passed. We waited. The hands on the clock moved ever so slowly. One minute swallowed up the next. Tension made us all smile too broadly and laugh too loudly.

No phone rang. No messenger gave reason. But the truth was finally clear. Carol had been stood up.

It was an elementary lesson in trust compared with the deeper challenges life has presented to Carol and the rest of us since that lonely night, but it has stayed with me, and I remember still the look of determination in her eyes as Carol chose her response.

With composure and wisdom beyond her natural maturity, my friend recited the promise she had memorized as a small Sunday school student, "No good thing will He withhold / From those who walk uprightly" (Psalm 84:11).

With just a bit of a quivering lip, Carol said, "This must not be good for me, and if it's not, then I surely don't want it!"

Direction-Correction-Protection

After sixteen years of marriage, Carol again felt the stab of rejection when, after mothering three children and working hard to put her husband through medical school, she lost her husband through divorce. The lessons learned at nine years of age and reaffirmed in her college years now became the anchor that helped her weather life's relentless storms. How has she survived? By developing a lifestyle of trust.

Think of your own disappointments. Now think of God's Word. Is it a point of victory for you? Have you discovered that the secret of contentment is trust?

"No good thing will He withhold." How marvelous it would be for our spiritual growth if we could once and for all claim His promise and apply it in every appropriate situation. How grand it would be if a lesson once learned could stay with us for life. Perhaps, though, we would be even more tempted to depend on ourselves and less on the Lord. So, He lovingly disciplines us with circumstances that challenge us to remember to trust Him more while we watch to see the puzzle come together.

As we watched Carol recover from her skirmish with self, we were all strengthened in our resolve to trust. Beginning that day, Carol's example planted a never-to-be-forgotten principle in our hearts and minds. It has grown and produced lasting fruit over the years when disappointments far greater have risen and weeds have tried to choke my own joy at the puzzles of circumstance.

In that time I have learned that His withholding gives

- Direction sometimes
- Correction at other times
- Protection all the time!

Remembering to trust teaches me that those who revere the Lord will not want for any good thing. They will, instead, be deeply grateful for all the good things received.

Learning to Remember to Trust

About twenty-five years ago we were in Connecticut, serving in a poverty pocket. Most of our congregation were experiencing the difficult reality of depending on the welfare system. It seemed that everything we touched and everywhere we looked were abundant opportunities to serve — more than we had strength or ability to cope with.

I became deeply discouraged when my health began to fail to the point that an ambulance whisked me to the hospital with a severe case of hepatitis.

"Lord, You know I don't have time for this!" I cried. "There is so much to be done, so many needs. Here I am, taking up a hospital bed, when there are worlds of people dying out there without You." I went on and on with my arguments and railed against the senselessness of being "shelved" for a season. After a very difficult year in our lives, knowing that my husband needed help with the ministry and our two small children couldn't fend for themselves, I was having a difficult time remembering to trust. Until one day the mail arrived and I opened an envelope to find a little piece of goldenrod stationery, folded in half, with a simple phrase and short story that revolutionized my life. The actual source of this story is unknown.

For This?

Many years ago in a small church in Ireland a minister gave a message that said that Jesus' words, "Abide in Me, and I in you," mean to simply say in every circumstance, "for this I have Jesus," and Jesus will say, "for this you have Me."

While the minister was speaking, the pianist received a telegram. It read: "Mother very ill, take first train home."

At the conclusion of the message she shared the telegram and added: "I've never traveled alone, but, 'for this I have Jesus.' I must cross the channel and make connections on the other side, but, 'for this I have Jesus.' Then I take a long train trip to the south of England, but, 'for this,' and all the suspense along the way, 'I have Jesus.' " As she spoke these words, the light of heaven could be seen upon her face.

Several weeks later a letter came from her. It was a song of praise. She wrote, "As I traveled that long, sorrowful journey, I continued to say, 'for this I have Jesus,' and He answered, 'for this you have Me.'

"As I reached home my sister fell sobbing on my shoulder saying, 'Oh, if you had come ten minutes sooner you would have seen Mother, who so longed to see you.' Instantly I looked up and said, 'for this I have Jesus,' and He came between me and my sorrow, and vain regrets had no power over me. We had never had a death or funeral in our family, and they all depended on me for every decision. Acknowledging my ignorance I said softly, 'for this I have Jesus,' and He gave me wisdom for every detail. There was also His perfect peace for all the legal matters that needed my attention.

"Now life has become joyous as in every circumstance I keep saying, 'for this I have Jesus.' "

The last paragraph of the little tract challenged me. "Christian reader," it said, "what is the circumstance in your life today that is beyond your control? Is it sorrow, sickness, suffering, fear, unsaved relatives, disappointments, discouragements, guidance, finances, misunderstandings, or another trial? You also can look into His face and say, 'for this I have Jesus,' and He will say, *'for this you have Me.'* "

He'll Finish the Puzzle

In my living room hangs a beautiful reminder. A dear woman needleworked those precious words and gave me the finished product as a gift. Perhaps you need to needlework those words or even put them on the dashboard of your car as I have. Maybe you could write them on a card and tuck it in your Bible, or, better yet, your wallet. Because when the money runs out, when there is no light at the end of the tunnel, when life is a complete puzzle — that's just the moment you need to remember to trust.

For this distracting, discouraging piece of the puzzle of my life, I have Jesus. What a touchstone. And what wonderful memorial words. Words to help me remember to trust God that someday I will be His *completed puzzle*.

Memo to myself:
   —*Memorize Psalm 84:11*
   —*Do a puzzle tonight*

Prayer:
   Thank You, Jesus, for being here, for whatever is before me today—or even tomorrow I have You and I am grateful. Amen.

Before I forget—I'll do it today:
   What "good" thing does God seem to be withholding from you? How can you show God that you trust Him with it today?
   Write down your three greatest worries today. For each, say and remember, "for this I have Jesus."

Chapter *11*

*R*emember the Children!

You must think constantly about these commandments I am giving you today. You must teach them to your children and talk about them when you are at home or out for a walk; at bedtime and the first thing in the morning.
(*Deut. 6:6-7 TLB*)

*M*aybe you'll relate to a new and fabulous drama in my life that is so amazing it has probably never happened to anyone else in the history of the world: *I became a grandmother*.

It may surprise you to know that I have pictures. Any time you want to see them, just stop by! After Emily's birth her proud mama (our daughter, Lois) gifted me with a beautifully bound Grandmother's Memory Book. In it is space for pictures of my own grandmother and even (if I could actually find one) my great-grandmother.

The pages, delicately edged in blue and white with pink accents, have room for remembrances of important historical events like bygone Christmas celebrations, how I met Emily's grandpa, places we visited when we were young; *everything* except how much I weigh and what I had for dinner last night.

Elegantly embossed on the front cover is my new name: "Grandmother Hepburn."

Legacy—a Treasured Responsibility

At first I ran my fingers over the raised lettering and thought, "What a treasure!" But an instant later a fretful inner voice countered, "Oh, my! What a responsibility!" I knew it could take months to assemble and write down all this information.

But I was willing, because, more than an heirloom, this pretty album can become the God-honoring gift of a "memorial stone." I sort of picture myself like old Joshua, getting those big rocks positioned in the Jordan River. He knew this exercise wasn't just a new aerobic activity. Joshua understood God's desire for solid reminders to guide future generations.

Who Cares About Teddy?

Elisabeth Elliot, author, speaker, and spiritual mentor, realized the importance of leaving a legacy. In 1971 she wrote to her mother, "Do me a favor, please. Go out and buy yourself a smallish loose-leaf notebook (five-by-eight or so) and start writing an autobiography. Put down, as they come to mind, all memories of your relatives, where and how they lived, what they wore; . . . smells, sounds, sights, menus, clothes, your dog, Teddy; . . . what happened when cars came in and horses went out. . . ."[1]

How grateful Elisabeth was when her mother responded. In fact she took it seriously enough to spend ten years working on her notebook. Pictures pasted, memories relived, it was like she had tasted life twice and created what her daughter describes as a "priceless document of a life that spanned the incredibly rapid progress from the horse-and-buggy to the moon walk, from gas lamps to electronics."[2]

Elisabeth's mother probably never imagined that anyone would care about her former habits or Teddy the dog. But those memories meant the world to her family. Just imagine for yourself how much richer you would be knowing about the lives of your grandparents or great-grandparents. Haven't you found yourself wondering what life was like for them? Or if they had the same struggles and questions you do?

Maybe you're reading this and you're a grandma. Why not start now? When you've gone on to glory, one or two young people might be impressed if you leave them an antique, some fancy trinkets, or a few dollars in your will. But, most likely, nothing will mean more than the written testimony of a grandma who loved and served the Lord.

If you're not in "prime time" yet, why not encourage an older relative? Purchase a cassette recorder, a blank book, or even some loose-leaf paper and an inexpensive photo album. Encourage the Joshuas in your family to remember to teach the children. If we don't teach them, what *will* they remember?

The Battle of Cherry Coke

A recent devotional story in the *Daily Bread* mentioned a preschooler whose rendition of "Joshua Fought the Battle of Jericho" lost something in the translation. Little Melissa sings instead, "Joshua fit the battle of Cherry Coke!" Isn't it easy to see how truth can be influenced by environment? Another child interpreted a verse of the "Battle Hymn of the Republic" by singing "He has trampled on the village where the great giraffe is stored!" Glory, hallelujah!

It's cute when children accidently switch around a few words. But if we don't make an effort to pass along God's truth accurately, words and values much more significant can be lost.

> Give ear, O my people, to my law;
> Incline your ears to the words of my mouth.
> I will open my mouth in a parable;
> I will utter dark sayings of old,
> Which we have heard and known,
> And our fathers have told us.
> We will not hide them from their children,
> Telling to the generation to come the praises of the
>   LORD,
> And His strength and His wonderful works that He has
>   done.
> For He established a testimony in Jacob,
> And appointed a law in Israel,
> Which He commanded our fathers,
> That they should make them known to their children ...
> That they may set their hope in God,
> And not forget the works of God....
>   (Ps. 78:1, 5, 7)

Do We Care?

A recent issue of Time ran a cover story: "Do We Care About Our Kids?" How shocking it was to read of the neglect and abuse so many young people bear. The article opens with a question you and I should ponder daily: "Just how much is a child worth?"[3]

The story tells of children in Thailand sold into prostitution and of those purchased in other countries for hard labor. Then the author hits home with statistics from our own country.

- Every twenty-six seconds a child runs away from home.
- Every forty-seven seconds a child is abused or neglected.
- Every sixty-seven seconds a teenager has a baby.
- Every seven minutes a child is arrested for a drug offense.
- Every thirty-six minutes a child is killed or injured by a gun.[4]

Without moral guidance and encouragement, our children will be left to "soak in whatever example their environment sets."[5]

Children are like sponges. They will soak up our values. That's why God commands us to teach the children His commands and holy practices now, before we forget.

It's not an option! Moses was talking to those who were about to enter the Promised Land without him. In fact, the book of Deuteronomy is a collection of five messages Moses gave to the children of Israel, knowing he would not be there to refresh their memories about all the important laws God had set down.

In the sixth chapter Moses tells them forcefully,

> These words which I command you today shall be in your heart. You shall teach them diligently to your children, and shall talk of them when you sit in your house, when you walk by the way, when you lie down, and when you rise up. You shall bind them as a sign on your hand, and they shall be as frontlets between your eyes. You shall write them on the doorposts of your house and on your gates.
>
> (Deut. 6:6-9)

Grandma's Fuzzy Mottoes

My grandma took that passage seriously. Grandma did not govern her house by the values of Better Homes and Gardens. In almost every room there were what I as a little girl called "fuzzy mottoes."

Each motto had a suede background (that's what made them fuzzy). There is one in my own home right now as a remembrance. I can picture them all over Grandma's house: *Prayer Changes Things*. My favorite one was Joshua 24:15: *As for Me and My House, We Will Serve the Lord.*

We never entered or left a room without having visually available to us the words and principles of God's Word, and I think about how Grandma did this so subtly — she probably didn't even know what subtle meant — and how we can, in simple ways, act upon this important law of God: We must not forget to teach the children.

The motto I have in my house is one that looks much like one I received when I was eight years old in a Sunday school promotion program in Syracuse, New York. We would attend Sunday school without fail for a full year for the presentation of a four-by-six fuzzy motto that said: *Lord, I Will Follow Thee.*

Can you imagine thinking that was a significant enough reward? But the value I learned was far more precious than even a trip to Disneyland. I'm grateful to my spiritual leaders who saw the importance of imparting God's truth to me. It has made all the difference in my life.

Practical Tools

Some creative ways for you to teach the children would be:

- A Promise Box — Write or type Bible promises on small cards and put them in a pretty jar, can, or box that you and the children can decorate. At meal times or prayer times or any time, pass the box around.
- Put Scripture cards in lunches.
- Keep magnets on the refrigerator with the verse of the week or the verse of the day.
- Assign a special verse on a birthday or holiday. Needlework it.

I had shared with a group of women the impact of 3 John 4 in my life. One of the women cross-stitched it for me and I have it framed and hanging in my living room: "I have no greater joy than to hear that my children walk in truth."

Behind Front Doors

I heard a very convicting question at a conference I attended.

"Which of your character qualities or habits would you most like your children to emulate?"

In that great group of women we all dropped our eyes, pondering just what it was that we would like our children to copy from our lives. Then she got really personal.

"Is it your hospitality? Is it your devotional life? Your service?"

Then I began to add to my own mental list: *Is it my sweet spirit under stress? Is it my willingness to be inconvenienced for others? Is it my prayer power that I would like my children to emulate?* Then she came back with these words, "Whatever it is, you *are* teaching them something."

The speaker was right. The most powerful teaching tool for

children is personal example. We can rationalize. We can excuse ourselves. But I believe our children have a God-given right to see their mothers walking a holy walk behind their own front doors. The most effective tool for teaching our children is our personal integrity.

I've started looking around in my home and in my life for things to fill the pages of the Memory Book my grandchildren will someday receive. I've copied down this prayer to be included as a reminder that, like my own grandma, I'm a fuzzy-motto kind of grandma. My motto is: Remember to teach the children. And to pray for them, too.

Father, hear us, we are praying,
Hear the words our hearts are saying,
We are praying for our children.

Keep them from the powers of evil,
From the secret, hidden peril,
Father, hear us for our children.

From the whirlpool that would suck them,
From the treacherous quicksand, pluck them,
Father, hear us for our children.

From the worldling's hollow gladness,
From the sting of faithless sadness,
Father, Father, keep our children.

Through life's troubled waters steer them,
Through life's bitter battle cheer them,
Father, Father, be Thou near them.

Read the language of our longing,
Read the wordless pleadings thronging,
Holy Father, for our children.

And wherever they may bide,
Lead them home at eventide.
                    Amy Carmichael[6]

Memo to myself:
    — Add to my Grandmother's Book
    — Buy refreshments for the neighbor's Good News Kid's Club
    — Take my turn at teaching a craft class at Juvenile Hall

Prayer:
    Lord, You love the children. Send Your angels to guard them. Amen.

Before I forget—I'll do it today:
    What memories passed to you have been helpful? To whom can you pass these today?
    What memory of yourself do you most want to pass on?

Chapter 12

Take Out the Garbage

Lord, who may abide in Your tabernacle?
Who may dwell on Your holy hill? . . .
He who swears to his own hurt and does not change.
(Ps. 15:1, 4)

*W*hen I was a young bride (a *very* young bride) I found myself a little overwhelmed when David and I were called to serve in a large children's home for dependent and neglected children. I had been raised in a secure Christian home, and it was hard to believe the conditions that innocent youngsters had to endure.

My heart would break every time I would look into the eyes of another child who had been victimized by parents or other adults. Sometimes it was more than I could take.

Children came to us by the dozens. Wards of the court. Some of them directly from juvenile hall. It was inconceivable to me thirty-five years ago and still is today that those wide-eyed youngsters could already have endured so much abuse and neglect. I will never forget the pain so evident behind the quivering lip of a disheveled little boy who slipped his hand into mine. Squeezing with all his frail might and looking desperately hopeful, he asked boldly, "Will you adopt me?"

It's a haunting memory when I think of all those children who have now produced another generation and another . . . all of them looking for a place to belong. As an officer of the Salvation Army, my father worked with alcoholics and those who were labeled "derelicts." Even though my home was a refuge, I was exposed through my father's ministry to the uglier side of life.

I saw clearly then that sin causes pain. It leaves wounded victims. Looking around at the end of the twentieth century, it isn't hard to see the effects of sin being visited upon the third and fourth generation.

Remember When?

Someone wrote:

> Do you remember when: The only hazard presented by insecticides was running into the flypaper . . . A marriage was likely to outlast all three wedding present toasters . . . A drug problem was trying to get a prescription filled on Sunday . . . The postman not only rang twice but also delivered twice . . . Bicycles and chickens came fully assembled . . . Paperbacks had more passion on the cover than in the contents . . . The quality of music wasn't measured in decibels . . . A whole family could go to the movies for what it now costs for a bag of popcorn?[1]

Those were the days, right? I am convinced that one reason marital discord, substance abuse, crime, and hot tempers are on the rise is because so few are willing to risk standing for righteousness. This is a personal soapbox. That's probably why my husband, David, has the unfortunate habit of introducing me as the "Chairman of the Universe."

He says it's because I seem to sense a more-than-average responsibility for keeping others accountable. Like shoplifters. If I see someone acting suspicious I'm compelled to do something about it. It's risky! But someone has to be brave!

Every now and then my antennas start beeping. Like the time in a department store when I noticed a devious-looking character slinking around behind the shoe display and peeking through the clothing racks.

"Miss, I think you ought to call security," I whispered crisply to the clerk.

"Ma'am," she whispered back with emphasis, "he *is* our security!"

So much for that. But I wasn't discouraged. I have not forgotten a promise I made to God fifteen years ago one evening following a city planning meeting. We were living in Minnesota at the time and our community leaders were deciding what to do about the entrance of pornography-for-profit into our community.

I'll never forget listening to a report from a woman on the city planning council and how I felt as I realized her point of view was far from what God's Word says about standing for righteousness.

"If you ever forget the Lord your God and follow other gods and worship and bow down to them, I testify against you today that you will surely be destroyed. Like the nations the Lord destroyed before you, so you will be destroyed for not obeying the Lord your God" (Deut. 8:19 NIV).

Many people attending the council meeting that night felt just as I did. "Why doesn't somebody do something?" I wondered. And that's when I knew in my heart that I was the one. You are the one. Each person is responsible for standing for righteousness within her own sphere of influence.

I promised the Lord that if He would grant me the strength, not a week would go by in which I didn't do at least one thing to be a part of the solution in a world gone crazy with unrighteousness. It's only by His grace that I can say I have kept my promise.

Recently I visited a novelty shop in San Francisco in lovely Ghirardelli Square and the presence of obscene and blasphemous Christmas cards caused me to speak out to confront obscenity. I visited the management of Ghirardelli Square and firmly suggested that the shops stop making those cards available. The women of our Bible study group and auxiliary and area churches generated scores of letters with as yet, little result.

The Right to Be Right

Am I disheartened? Who wouldn't be? Will I consider my efforts a waste of time? Absolutely not! Magnetized to my refrigerator is a memo scripted with this marvelous quote by Thornton Wilder:

> You say the little efforts that I make
> Will do no good; they never will prevail
> To tip the hovering scale
> Where justice hangs in balance.
> I don't think

> I thought they ever would.
> But I am prejudiced beyond debate
> In favor of my right to choose which side
> Shall feel the stubborn ounces of my weight.

Why don't you read it one more time for emphasis? It means so much to me. Remember this: You and I might not be able always to effect change in others; but we can keep others from changing us. And that's important because we can all be deeply influenced by our environment. Here's an example.

House-blind

In a column for the Providence Journal, Mark Patinkin painted a word picture about what can happen if we don't do something to get rid of the garbage around us. His title, "House-blindness: If it's been there long enough, it isn't there," demonstrates what can happen when we coexist with garbage.

According to Patinkin, this "classic American illness" occurs when we get comfortable with something that originally repulsed us. He said when new homeowners move into a house and hate the green wallpaper or orange carpeting they'll vow to rip it out. But if they don't do it within a month, it's too late because they don't see it anymore.

"I've suffered from house-blindness for years," he writes. "In my last house I had a habit of putting garbage bags in the dining room. I once missed four garbage days in a row, and the dining room ended up filled with fifteen bags.

" 'What are we going to do about these garbage bags?' Heidi finally asked.

" 'What garbage bags?' I said."[2]

Think of all the garbage we have tolerated for so long in our society. We take it for granted. We feel pressured to live with it. We are no longer shocked by it. We are house-blind.

It's Nothing New

Nothing's really changed. Moses said the same thing to the Israelites.

> When you have eaten and are full, then you shall bless the LORD your God for the good land which He has given you. Beware that you do not forget the LORD your God by not keeping His commandments, His judgments, and His statutes which I command you today, lest—when you have eaten and are full, and have built beautiful houses and dwell in them; . . . when your heart is lifted up, and you forget the LORD your God who brought you out of the land of Egypt, from the house of bondage . . . then you say in your heart, "My power and the might of my hand have gained me this wealth."
>
> And you shall remember the LORD your God, for it is He who gives you power to get wealth.
>
> (Deut. 8:10-12, 14, 17-18)

Do you hear it in that passage? It's the message of a secular, high-tech, New Age philosophy: "We've done it ourselves. We are the creators—the 'gods.' So, any problem we have, we can solve. With a little bit of consciousness raising we can clean up our planet if we all save enough plastic bottles or put up enough 'No smoking' signs."

Who Dropped the Ball?

Retraining the mindset of a society that has forgotten its source will be the most difficult moral duty of our day. Like the Israelites, we must pledge: "We will tell the next generation the praiseworthy deeds of the Lord — his power and the wonders he has done. He decreed statutes. . . ."

The statutes are laws, a frame of reference for how we are to propagate what we have been given. He decreed statutes, He commanded our forefathers — even the children yet to be born — and they in turn would tell their children. . . .

What happened? Somewhere along the way we've dropped the ball. I often speak on the topic "Moral Issues of the '90s" at seminars. When I do I carry with me the January 1990 issue of *Moody Monthly* magazine. After conducting a poll, the editors came up with nine of the most urgent issues of this decade. One of the issues highlighted was "The Agony in the City: We Are Losing Our Children," in which a speaker was quoted as saying, "We may simply have to give up on this generation of kids and work for the future of the next generation."[3]

After listening to two pastors, a psychiatrist, the chief of police, a lawyer, and other community leaders, the author says, "I had never seen the group so discouraged or feeling so helpless."[4]

Is it really too late to rescue the teens that are now in our homes and schools?

Moody editor Joseph Stowell poses an interesting thought: "Our forefathers established an America rooted in trust in God, His Word, and His ways. We have witnessed in our lifetimes the death of that dream and the dawning of secularism. Why did we change our minds?"

Our minds were changed when, in our prosperity, we forgot the Lord. As a person "thinks in his heart, so is he" (Prov. 23:7). Stowell says, "Making up our minds ultimately makes up our lives."[5]

Making up our minds to remember the Lord and get rid of garbage in our personal lives and in society can be costly. For my friend June, the cost was great, but so was the harvest.

"You're in Jail?"

I received a phone call from a friend and prayer partner. "Daisy, we've got to pray for June!" June had attended a Hope of Our Heritage conference ten years ago where she committed to make a moral difference in her community. June is my age — it's the age I call "Prime Time" because women in this forty–to–seventy–year age group are freer and more available to serve the Lord than ever before.

June is the wife of a pediatrician. And available. She almost single-handedly put the Josh McDowell sex education course into her local high-school district. That was one place she felt she could make a moral difference.

On the phone that day my prayer partner Lois said, "Daisy, we've got to pray for June. She's in jail!"

June had been sentenced to forty-five days in a Los Angeles jail for her participation in Operation Rescue. I did send her notes and arranged prayer support. After two weeks I called to ask her husband how she was doing in jail. June answered the phone!

"June, what are you doing home? You're supposed to be in jail!"

"I got released yesterday," she told me. "Nobody serves a full sentence anymore. The jails are so overcrowded that whether you're a robber or a rapist, a murderer or a pickpocket, you get out early. That's how overloaded the judicial system is."

"How did you survive?" I asked. I had dreary images in my mind and was terribly curious about what this fragile little lady had experienced.

"Well it was better this year than last," she said with a smile in her voice.

"What?" I was shocked. "June! You mean to tell me you were in jail last year, too?"

"Yes, and it was much easier this year. You see, I was put into a cell block with about one hundred and fifty other women. We had drug pushers, prostitutes, and everything you could imagine. It was quite an experience. As soon as they checked me in I was assigned to help in the infirmary. I prayed, 'Okay, Lord, here I am. In some way, Lord, get glory. Make it count.' I had no idea how long I'd be there."

Do you know what the Lord did for her? He helped her see that she had resources the one hundred and forty-nine other women didn't.

"I had prayed to be used by God. Then when I realized that I was going to be living with more needy women, more women in desperate circumstances, more women open to answers than God could have given me in two or three years of my own efforts of going out and trying to witness for Him. I said 'Thank You, Lord!'

"I realized I had something I didn't have before. I had *time*.

And I had a captive audience. I decided to make that time count. I have prayed with, talked to, and have addresses for more opportunities than I can handle. In fact, right now I'm making muffins to take to the jail."

Be Prepared

There was such a message in June's life. Be prepared. It challenged me. If June had not been preparing herself for service, she could have responded with bitterness, sorrow, and self-pity, which are more common reactions to bad circumstances. What helped her respond with joy to a jail sentence? What can help me react positively to whatever my day brings? Being prepared.

Here are five ways we can be prepared for the good works of service that Ephesians 2:10 tells us God created us for.

1. Pray that God will use you: "Lord, You know my talents, my abilities, and my limitations. I give them to you. Be glorified by the way I live. Use the me You created."

2. Cultivate a willing heart—by responding immediately in obedience when you see a need you can meet or a good work you can perform. Write a letter to the newspaper editor or your government representative to help change or initiate a law.

3. Be alert to life: Look around you. It's often true that we see only what we want to see or we get so caught up in our own problems that we don't look outward. Take time to read the newspaper. Are there victims from a fire? One man I know read in the paper that a family lost their home just before Christmas. He quietly

went out and bought gifts for the children and made a real difference.

4.   Expect God to use you. He will!

5.   Practice righteousness. Every day we face choices. Choose righteousness.

I had such an opportunity one day when, following the borrowed pickup my husband was driving, I tried to heed his instructions to honk three times if there was any kind of emergency. This was an emergency!

After two or three miles of honking, David finally pulled over.

"One of the rubbish bags fell off the truck a couple of exits back!" I shouted to him through my car window. "It was probably just some old linens. Let's not go back. I just want to get home."

David insisted we go back, however, so we turned around and tried to locate the missing bag.

Can you picture, along the freeway, trees bedecked with pink fluff from bed pillows and shrubbery draped with bed sheets? I pulled over and sat, laughing, while my husband collected our belongings before anyone we knew happened by.

Soon a stranded motorist approached my car and expressed relief that help had arrived. He said that his van had come to an abrupt halt when it ran over a plastic bag, which was now firmly affixed to the underside of this vehicle, cutting his gas tank and causing other damage to his van. Immediately, we owned up to our responsibility.

The bid on his repair work arrived later. For what we paid to have his van fixed, we could have redecorated our bedroom several times over with new linens! Why did we have to go back?

"Thank you for your good faith," the motorist said, as we wrote the check to cover the damage to his van.

"Good faith?" I argued with my old nature. "Lots of people drop things on the freeway and never even know it. Why did we have to go back? Why, the guy could probably have just turned the damage in to his own insurance company."

Sometimes it hurts to accept responsibility. Sometimes it's not what "lots of people" do — choosing righteousness. But that's one way we can be prepared for what God calls us to do.

What's God getting you ready for? He's got more for you than simply a status-quo passivity.

Are we serious about remembering the Lord? Are we willing to take out the garbage and not become house-blind?

It's fascinating to me how we operate as Christian women. Think about it. We get together for fellowship in our churches and on retreats and pray for missions . . . we raise money and hope it will help . . . we go to work days for missions if it's at our convenience.

God has a sense of humor. Do you know what He is doing? He has lifted up a whole Asian community and deposited it in our area. He has lifted up the equivalent of a large Hispanic city and deposited it at the doorstep of the churches of our city. God has said, "This is the time to put your hands and feet and mouth where your heart has been."

It is going to become increasingly inconvenient to serve the Lord. We're going to have to be "on call," giving patient instruction; helping the Vietnamese woman with a driver's license questionnaire; taking the Hispanic woman grocery shopping because she can't speak English. That's what it's going to take. It's going to take you and me throwing open the doors of our churches and hearts. To be available.

It's going to take us believing our children aren't hopelessly lost. It's going to take us remembering the statutes of the Lord. Taking out the garbage. Not allowing ourselves to become house-blind.

Memo to myself:
   — Take the baby clothes and diapers we collected and drop them off at the crisis pregnancy center
   — Write a letter to the TV sponsors in appreciation for the great program we enjoyed last night
   — Clear the clutter from the kitchen counter

Prayer:
   Lord, are there blind spots in my life? Please search me, O God, and see if there is any wicked way in me. Create in me a clean heart. Amen.

Before I forget—I'll do it today:
   How can you contribute to the cause of righteousness in your neighborhood today?
   To what habits or items have you become house-blind?
   Are you faithful to pass on the "praiseworthy deeds of the Lord"?

Do you know someone who might need your help but may be too shy to ask for it?

Chapter 13

Don't Forget to Pray

Yes, I will bless the Lord and not forget the glorious things He does for me.
(Ps. 103:2 TLB)

*D*o you count on your memory? Does it come through when you really need it? It is comforting to be assured that we can count on the Lord to jog our memories. I saw this clearly when a young woman in Washington state told me about her grandfather-in-law.

He had Alzheimer's disease—this man who had been known in younger years for his quick wit and attention to detail. He had been a minister. Respected. Dependable. Now he was confined to a nursing home. His children and grandchildren would visit regularly. Family photos were displayed in his modest room, yet there was no indication that Grandpa Eric even knew who they were.

Until it was time to go; then someone would say, "Grandpa, would you pray with us?" and he would stretch out a feeble hand, eager to begin. When he prayed, something mysterious happened. Grandpa remembered names and circumstances as he lifted his loved ones before the throne of grace.

It brought tears to my eyes, because I had known Eric Newbould personally, and it gave me great comfort and encouragement to know that when physical limitations caused him to forget so much, the God he loved and served *reminded him to pray*.

In all the confusion of his deteriorating life, remembering to pray brought stability and inner healing.

With Prayer, We Win

Isn't it good to know we serve a God who is able to penetrate the barriers of our human limitations? Prayer is a powerful tool in the life of the believer. Lois Johnson, a friend and author in Minneapolis, was commissioned to write a book on her pilgrimage of prayer. During the process of researching and writing the book, Lois received a shocking and horrendous diagnosis. She had cancer.

And so the book that she wrote took two tracks. Though it dealt heavily with her ever-enriching experience of communicating with the Lord in her prayer life, right alongside was her painful pilgrimage through the treatment and eventual cure for her cancer. She writes, "Someone who prayed with me once asked, 'Lois, how can you thank God before you even see the answer?' "

And after thinking a moment, she replied, "Often I thank God out of the knowledge of past experiences, knowing that God will perform His work because He is faithful, and at other times I thank out of trust because of what He has promised."[1]

The title she gave her finished book was *Either Way I Win!* What a good reminder!

Practicing Prayer

What is prayer? I address women all the time who are under

such a burden of guilt because they don't have a measured amount of time — like fifteen minutes or an hour — with the Lord every day. My personal goal for including a chapter on prayer in this book about remembering is to encourage practical praying. We've got to move past legalism. Otherwise prayer can become such a source of discouragement.

Brother Lawrence, a fifteenth-century monk known for his deep love of God, wrote about his prayer life. In his classic book, *The Practice of the Presence of God*, he explained that prayer is simply sensing the presence of God. He made a habit of allowing his soul to become insensitive to everything but divine love.

He wrote, "The time of business does not with me differ from the time of prayer; and in the noise and clatter of my kitchen, while several persons are at the same time calling for different things, I possess God in as great tranquility as if I were upon my knees at the blessed sacrament."[2]

I don't know about you, but that concept means a great deal to me. Just the fact that you're reading this book means you probably face many distractions and pressures that pull you away from spending time remembering the Lord. Like me, you probably have appointments, financial burdens, relatives who need your personal care and attention, families who are dependent upon your services, neighbors for whom you are concerned, friends in need of quality time, church challenges, volunteer organizations — and that's only the tip of the iceberg!

Praying on the Run

How do we keep our prayer lives afloat in the midst of life's demands? We must develop practical ways of practicing prayer.

When we lived in Puerto Rico, our son was seven years old. One day his friend came rushing into our house crying and screaming, *"David un golpe grande!"* Translated: "A great, big wound!" David had had an accident.

Without hesitation I rushed out to see that our youngster had fallen out of a tree. I could tell by the amount of blood that his leg needed immediate attention, and I scooped him up and headed for the doctor. It may seem unspiritual to some, but I did not stop for a word of prayer.

Sometimes you've just got to pray on the run. After the stitches and the doctor who made himself available and the agony that was relieved for my son and myself, I was thankful for the God who hears whether I'm calm and focused or frantic and scurrying.

While appointed times of prayer are important and bring our faith into focus, we also have to learn how to pray on the run. Don't you agree? Here are a few creative ways to fold prayer into a busy schedule:

- *Prayer Visors*. In Tacoma, Washington, a creative pastor devised a plan for reminding his congregation to pray. He created clever cards that fit the visors in automobiles. The cards are distributed monthly with an appropriate verse of Scripture, names of missionaries, needs within the church, community needs, and so on. All the prayer requests are copied on the card in punchy bright letters so that even at a red light, the driver can turn down the visor and spend a moment or two breathing a name or need to the Lord. What a wonderful, simple way to practice the Presence.

- *Handprints*. I am often asked this piercing question:

"Daisy, how can I influence grandchildren who are being raised in a home that is not putting Christ first?" Recently a gracious lady shared this wonderful idea with me. She said, "I have ten grandchildren and I have bought this plain spiral notebook. I call it my Prayer Notebook. At the top of each page I've written the name of one of my grandchildren. As I hear of special things I need to remember to pray for them, I note them on their pages.

"When I see them, however, I ask each one to place one hand on his or her page, and I draw around it. Every morning when I kneel by my bed, I open my Notebook before the Lord. As I name the children, I put my hand on each one's handprint and say, 'Lord, please make this grandmother a link in the spiritual life and growth of this child.'"

- *'Round-the-clock Prayers.* Karen Barber in Dun-woody, Georgia, said that while teaching a ninth-grade Sunday school class she searched for a way to remember each student in prayer during the week. She handed out index cards and asked the students to write down what parts of the day were most difficult for them — the times they thought a little extra grace to get through would be helpful. Everyone began writing. Karen said four of them had a hard time getting up in the morning and dreaded it. She propped the cards near her own alarm so she'd remember them each morning.

Some mentioned certain class periods at school. Those cards went on the clock in Karen's office. On and on they went until Karen had prayer reminders " 'round the clock."

- *Prayer-by-association*. My friend Jan, a Bible teacher, has a real spiritual commitment to the women in her class. Just naming names at the beginning of the day didn't seem effective enough. Then God gave her the idea of praying by association. One woman's son has a kidney disease. If this boy is unable to drink enough water to flush out his system, he will become fatally ill. So Jan decided that every time she turned on the faucet or took a drink of water she would pray for little Steven.

  Think of the ways this could be adapted in your own life. One woman prays for her son while sorting his socks. Vacuuming the living room could remind us to pray for our children's purity and the cleansing of our own hearts. "Search me, O God, and know my heart," the psalmist wrote. We could pray, "Vacuum all the dusty impurities out of my heart, Lord!"

- *Prayer Rocks*. A fun thing someone gave me is a prayer rock. It's just a little pebble wrapped up in a pretty square of fabric with a satin ribbon tying it to a card that reads:

  > I'm just a little prayer rock and this is what I do:
  > Drop me on your pillow and when the day is through
  > Turn back the covers and climb in bed . . .
  > Whack! The little prayer rock will hit you in the head.
  > Then you will remember, when the day is through
  > To kneel and say your prayers, just as you wanted to.
  > Then when the day is over, drop me on the floor

Where I stay all night to give you help once more.
First thing up next morning, whoops! You'll stub a toe
You're surely to remember prayers before you go.
Drop me on your pillow when your bed is made
Your handy little rock will continue to your aid.
Because your heavenly Father cares and loves you so,
He wants you to remember to talk to Him, you know.

• *Prayer Triplets*. Millie Dienert teaches women all over the world to pray in threes. Each woman chooses the names of three unsaved friends or relatives. Then the group meets regularly to pray for the salvation of those nine individuals. What an encouragement to see God answer!

Prayer Worriers

Major Della Rees said laughingly that a virus in the computers caused the typographical error in a church newsletter. Instead of Prayer Warriors, the article talked about "Prayer Worriers." I had to ask myself the question, am I a prayer worrier? There's an old saying: Why worry when you can pray? How often it's turned around: Why pray when you can worry?

Prayer soldiers report for duty knowing the equipment and resources will be there. Prayer worriers show up, but they're full of doubt.

Major Rees pointed out in a column that there are two reasons most people choose to practice worrying instead of praying.

1. We really don't believe God.
2. We really don't want to give God control.[3]

When the apostle Peter was in prison, his friends gathered to pray. They are an example of prayer worriers who don't believe God can do what we ask of Him. Do you remember that when Peter was miraculously released from prison, they said, "No, it must be his ghost!" The girl who answered the door when Peter knocked slammed it in his face in disbelief! And that was after they had been praying all night he would be freed!

What are you worrying over that you can't believe God for? Is there too much month at the end of your money? Is that rocky relationship going to break apart? Is the doctor's report for your aging parent going to mean you will have to share your already crowded home?

Is the phone ever going to ring with good news? Right now I'm waiting to hear from my precious daughter whose due date was yesterday. We live hundreds of miles apart. This will be my second grandchild. Will Lois be all right? Will the baby have ten fingers and toes? Will the delivery be smooth? Will the baby come before I have to leave on an extended trip to fulfill several commitments?

I know God can provide. He can heal broken hearts and help us find inner strength for the moment. He can help you manage that sickly older parent. He can see my Lois through the challenge of childbirth. But we must believe Him. We must report for prayer duty as warriors instead of worriers.

When we choose to practice anxiety in place of practicing prayer we prove that we want to be the "captains of our own fate." In Philippians 4:6-7, Paul tells us not to be anxious about anything but instead to pray, give thanks and receive God's peace. Major Rees adds that the passage describes four ways to be a prayer warrior:

1. Don't worry needlessly.

2. Come to God with praise and thanksgiving.

3. Tell God everything that is on your mind.

4. Rest in the peace you have through the Lord Jesus Christ.[4]

"I sought the LORD and He heard me, / And delivered me from all my fears" (Ps. 34:4).

Learning to practice the presence of God is a survival mechanism for these last days. I need to be aware of the presence, the covering, the protection, and the direction of God throughout my day.

We are all faced with a day full of impossibilities, improbabilities, challenges, and interruptions. We need to have that deep, settled sense of His presence within. It only comes with practice.

More Prayer

Many, many days as I was growing up I would wake up in the morning and pad my way downstairs, sleepy-eyed, and see Daddy sitting in the room nearest the kitchen before he took the trip to work. He would be there each morning without fail—praying. To think that I had a father who prayed for me every day of my life—what a privilege!

It was something to behold. Something I cherish. After Daddy went to heaven, I talked with Colonel Lyle Rader, a dear gentleman who shared a prayer fellowship with my father. There were seven men in their group and they were known as "The Praying

Seven." Their mission as prayer warriors was to intercede for and uphold the work of the Salvation Army.

"I'm going to miss my dad," I told Colonel Rader. "I'm going to miss his prayers for me."

That's when Lyle Rader said something I'll never forget. Intercessory prayer is a beautiful mystery, and I don't think we'll fully understand it until we see Jesus face to face. But this rhetorical response has stayed in my heart, comforting me and reminding me that true prayer is really practicing God's presence.

When I said to this dear man of prayer, "I'm going to miss my daddy's prayers for me," he asked, "Daisy, do you think there will be less prayer in heaven?"

Hungry for Prayer?

Why should we remember to pray? Besides the obvious benefits of answered prayer and inner peace, Billy Graham points out the importance of obedience: "The Christian should have an appetite for prayer. He should want to pray. One does not have to force food upon a healthy child. Exercise, good circulation, health and labor demand food for sustenance. So it is with those who are spiritually healthy. They have an appetite for the Word of God, and for prayer."

Prayer unites us with God. Sin separates us from God. When the mischievous little girl got into her mother's lipstick and the mother asked, "Debbie, what did you do?" Debbie said, "I don't want to talk about it!"

We don't feel like talking to God, either, when our fellowship is broken. Mr. Graham says, "If you do not feel like praying, it is probably a good indication that you should start praying immediately."

Don't forget to remember the glorious things God has done. Don't forget to practice the presence of God. And in case you're tempted to be a prayer worrier, just remember Grandpa Eric. Count on God. And don't forget to pray.

Memo to myself:
— Get Emily's little handprint impressed in my prayer notebook
— Find my old prayer rock . . . make another one to place under my pillow

Prayer:
Lord, remind me to pray out of Your promises. Make me hungry for prayer and filled with Your Spirit of trust. Amen.

Before I forget—I'll do it today:
Stop this minute and check your heart. What worries you today? Before you forget—pray.

Chapter 14

Remember What You Learned at Home

O LORD, You are the portion of my inheritance and my cup;
You maintain my lot.
The lines have fallen to me in pleasant places;
Yes, I have a good inheritance.
(Ps. 16:5-6)

*M*aybe you'll see me on *America's Funniest Home Videos*. No kidding! I sent a tape. If I win first place, the money will fund our next family reunion. Our theme will be: "It pays to remember what you learned at home!"

Last August, fifty-eight family members met in a conference center in the beautiful rolling, green hills of Pennsylvania. My four sisters, our husbands, children, and grandchildren from thirteen states spent four lovely days together. Within our group we have seven preachers. Can you believe it?

What crazy fun we had! We performed a family circus, played Family Feud, drummed up a family band and choir, and listened as my distinguished brother-in-law, the "senior" pastor of the clan, preached on Sunday. He reminded us that the Lord had directed our family along pleasant places. Our children and grandchildren listened, wide-eyed, as he spoke of the heritage of godly, praying grandparents that some of our children had never even met.

How our hearts were warmed and encouraged. Tears flowed as Uncle Henry told about Grandma and Grandpa, especially when he remembered how they prayed that God would raise up children after them to love and trust and faithfully serve the Lord.

Memories Compensate

Memories are such a healing balm. That's why Psalm 103:2 says "Bless the LORD, O my soul, / And forget not all His benefits." I just learned today that the Hebrew word for "benefit" can also be translated "recompense" or "compensation for things suffered." A celebration of our memories can make up for the sorrow of loss and help us move on with joy.

When I think of Uncle Henry's message at our reunion, the idea of compensation rings true. He reminded us of some of the humorous things that took place in Grandma and Grandpa's home. One we'll never forget was Grandpa's love for popcorn. When all of us kids would go to visit their retirement home in the endless mountains of Pennsylvania, a very important ritual would take place. Grandpa would get out the old popcorn popper. Bushels of popcorn later, everyone would be laughing, playing, and making memories.

There were also games of dominoes and hide-and-seek and other ways to pass the time, but popcorn was our sacred ritual. I've often stood at my microwave in recent days experiencing a wash of warm emotions as the Orville Redenbacher bag swells.

And I think about how my dad would have been fascinated to have that much popcorn made in three-and-a-half minutes!

Yet none of us would trade the charm of my daddy standing there wanting to please his children and grandchildren, stirring that old popcorn popper. Orville Redenbacher can't hold a candle to the memories I have of that time and how my daddy longed to hold his grandchildren on his knee, make them laugh, and pray with them to pass along a heritage of faith and love.

Big Bird's Funny Video

Uncle Henry's moving sermon was a tribute, a memorial stone, a compensation to be tucked away in the corners of our minds. His message was profound and moving. That's probably what made our videocassette recording even more hilarious later when we reviewed the scene you may someday view on national TV. (Don't laugh! I'm serious!) Remember I told you we had a Family Circus? It was my sister's idea.

Each clan was responsible for producing a circus act. We had clowns. We had a circus band in place. We had a popcorn vendor, of course. Each family was assigned a color and we had matching T-shirts. My sister Jane had the largest population in offspring, and they performed a lion tamer's act. Her kids wore lion and tiger hats. They even jumped through hoops.

Doris's family did a takeoff on *Sesame Street*. They called it *Doris Drive*. It was so clever! The videotape was rolling. How thankful we are for modern technology! Doris's six-foot, five-inch husband, Henry-the-preacher, was a natural to play Big Bird.

He was elaborately regaled in a yellow feathered wig. They

put a beak on him, dressed him up with huge, round, yellow plastic table cloths for wings, and underneath it all had him poured into white tights to get the skinny, bird-leg effect. Take a minute here. You have to understand. This is my brother-in-law. Dignified. Quiet. A Presbyterian pastor for many years, but willing to do anything for the good of the family.

It was funny enough just looking at Henry. We could hardly contain ourselves. That's why it was a scream when it happened. First the "wings" slipped slightly. Henry was making the introductions for the cast of *Doris Drive*. But as he reached to pull up the sleeve, the tablecloth gave way and in an instant with kind of a swooshing sound, our staid Dutchman preacher was standing unraveled and bird-legged! The yellow plastic was a cloud at his feet. It brought the house down — needless to say. And it's all on film. No one would believe it otherwise.

We Need Each Other

The joy and tears of our reunion will be long remembered. That's how it should be. One of my nieces made a special presentation about remembering our roots. We received beautifully crafted photo albums as a treasured reminder of that gathering. To me it's also a recollection of something deeper: We need each other. We need memorial stones and touchstones that bring us together, for they are compensations for the yesterdays left behind. They remind us of God's benefits.

Things Never Forgotten

My friend Barbara Johnson mails out a regular newsletter. In a recent issue she published the following:

Twelve Things You'll Never Forget

1. The spanking or scolding you thought you didn't deserve.

2. Your first night alone or away from your family.

3. An early grade card filled with A's . . . or F's.

4. Your first kiss.

5. The play you made that decided the game in your team's favor.

6. The simple joys of picking wild violets or gathering hickory nuts with a grandparent.

7. The day you were ill and allowed to miss school and you had strawberry ice cream.

8. The first time you slept in a tent.

9. Holidays with all the relatives joking, laughing and eating.

10. The loss of a special person.

11. Catching "lightning bugs" and putting them in a bottle.

12. The harsh words you spoke — and now regret.[1]

Do those bring back memories for you? Each one brought a different essence to my memory sensors. Dear Barbara, who has suffered so much loss in her family, was asked on a national radio program why she thought her son had returned to God and his home from a wayward lifestyle after eleven years. In Barbara's books and through her teaching and speaking ministry, she has encouraged thousands of parents with the hope that prodigals do return.

"What I really believe," Barbara replied, "is that there were spiritual resources planted deep in Larry's heart. He had learned well at home."

It's Cool in the Furnace

"It pays to remember what you learned at home!"[2] The young campers sang as loud as they could. The song was a selection from "It's Cool In The Furnace," a musical production at the junior camp week in middle Minnesota. Our theme for the week was taken from the book of Daniel. The dramatic musical performance was going to be the culmination of that camp experience.

How enthusiastically those kids sang. We had lived in "Babylon" all week long. Each cabin was transformed into a lion's den. The dining hall became the King's palace, where we reenacted the scene of the mysterious handwriting on the wall by using lemon juice and a blow torch. Daniel himself was present in the person of our assistant camp director.

Day and night we creatively experienced Daniel's world. Once we even tried to escape Babylon as the children of Israel. It was the middle of the night when the campers roused and trekked across the beach and lawn only to be interrupted by the "King" himself. So we had to return to our homes....

The next morning on the way to the mailbox, I couldn't help chuckling when I read what one young camper had written on a postcard to home:

> Dear Mom,
> Daisy made us go on a ten mile hike. We tried to run away, but King Ezzerkineezer caught us. Please come on Sunday.
> Love, Suzie

I wonder what her mother thought! Those young people learned that week that when King Nebuchadnezzar attacked Jerusalem he ordered his soldiers to take some fine young Jewish men and bring them back as captives. " "Pick strong, healthy, good-looking lads,' " he said; " "those who have read widely in many fields, are well informed, alert and sensible, and have enough poise to look good around the palace' " (Dan. 1:4 TLB).

One of those young men was Daniel. Surely King Nebuchadnezzar felt that once he got Daniel away from his home he could change him into the kind of slave he wanted. But the Bible tells us that "Daniel purposed in his heart that he would not defile himself" (Dan. 1:8). I can't help thinking about his mama. Maybe she was a thousand miles away from Babylon, where her young son now lived. Maybe she wasn't even alive anymore. Whatever the circumstances, she could never have known how powerfully her early input in Daniel's life would impact his future.

Daniel, as a young teen, had nothing and no one holding him accountable except the convictions his mother had built into his life. Undoubtedly he remembered that the Jewish laws he had learned were still valid even though the temptations in the palace must have been appealing. Daniel remembered what he had learned at home. He knew how to pray. Most importantly, he had learned to look at God, not at the lions in life.

Over the years, his life gave evidence that godly values, learned early, are foundation stones that support well the walls of strong character.

An Inheritance

What is your heritage? What will you leave behind for those you love? Psalm 16:6 refers to the gifts our Father has given us when the psalmist exclaims, "What a wonderful inheritance!" (TLB). Will those you leave be able, like Daniel, to benefit from what they learned at home? I often ask myself those kinds of questions these days. I'm sixty years old. At my age, it's not unusual to think of my beneficiaries. What treasures will they have?

The other day I drove by a hand-painted sign. *Estate Sale*, it read in bold, black letters. An arrow underneath pointed the way. Of course, I couldn't resist. Occasionally I can pass up an ordinary garage sale because yard and garage sales usually consist of leftover bric-a-brac and unwanted stuff. On the other hand, estate sales usually feature the treasures, the important keepsakes left after the owners have passed on.

As I wandered through the house, picking up a glass vase here and a tarnished picture frame there, I couldn't help wondering what my own estate sale would be like. If someone pulled out the contents from the back corner of my bedroom closet, would they be keepsakes? Are my treasures purely of earthly value? I've got to admit that I resolved right then and there to clean my closets!

Just the thought of someone wading through all the jumble in my storage places made me shudder! But more than that, I determined to spend more time laying up treasures in heaven. For as lovely as some of the knickknacks and handmade quilts and antique tables were at the sale, they only served to remind me that lasting riches are the ones we stock in heaven.

Mama's Home Treasures

That's a truth my mama was sure her daughters learned. I look around my home right now and I see evidences of my mother and dad's home. The light fixture above my dining room table is one Mama found at a yard sale in the hills of Pennsylvania. I understand it belonged in a very polished, old-fashioned railroad car. Mama was so tickled to find it. It suited her personality perfectly and for years it decorated their retirement home before it became mine.

There are not a lot of other treasures. I've got a beautiful lamp that Mother found in a second-hand store. Hanging on one wall is a bed warmer with its old copper basin that could use a touch of polish and some elbow grease. But as I look around, I think of the treasures they left and I remember the greatest legacy

Mama left: the example that says there are no *real* treasures in this earth. It's so simple.

So estate sales make me wonder, what will be left when we leave our home?

Estate sales have items that were once precious parts of people's hearts and lives. My niece is working on a tribute to Mama's desire to leave behind the most important kinds of treasures. Every week, year after year, Mama would sit down with ten sheets of onion skin typing paper, some carbon inserts, and her very old, but ever-faithful Smith-Corona typewriter. Then she would compose a newsletter for our family. We always gave Mama rolls of stamps for Christmas. Now my niece is compiling those old letters and having them bound in book form. What a treasure. What memories of our home and our heritage.

Mama was so dear. She had an unquenchable curiosity about the lives of her five daughters after they moved away from her. I remember when David and I purchased a home in the Santa Cruz mountains. Knowing that she'd probably never make it out from Pennsylvania to see exactly how we lived, Mama hovered over her typewriter and put together a detailed questionnaire, complete with carbon copies, and sent it for me to fill out.

When the mailman delivered it I sat down and really giggled to think that Mama couldn't trust me to describe all the important things. She left room between the questions for my type-written answers:

Q. Do you have two bathrooms?

A. Two and a half; one cute half-bath inside front door.

Q. Is your living room long or square?

A. About twenty-two feet long, with stairs with open railing at one end to second floor.

Q. Dishwasher?

A. Yes.

Q. Can two eat in the kitchen?

A. No!

Etc., etc. . . .

I had some kind of Mama!

Two years ago I was in a shop across the bay and there sitting in a corner was a tarnished plaque. The faded blue background was surrounded with a gilt-edged frame in need of polishing. As I picked it up and read a phrase from Mama's favorite hymn, I could almost hear her humming:

Earth Has No Sorrow That Heaven Cannot Heal.

That plaque now hangs in my bedroom. Still tarnished, but shining with truth I learned in my Mama and Daddy's home. It's a treasure of truth — one that you can't buy at an estate sale.

Samuel Webbe wrote the words to the hymn represented on that old plaque. He wrote them in the 1700s, but they still ring true in my heart as they did in Mama's:

Come, ye disconsolate, where'er ye languish;
Come to the mercy seat, fervently kneel;

Here bring your wounded hearts, here tell your anguish;
Earth has no sorrow that heaven cannot heal.

The old lamp, bed warmer, typewriter, and other tangible items my parents left behind probably wouldn't bring much at an estate sale. Like all the keepsakes in the back of my closets, they'll someday be sold or taken and stored away by loved ones or just tossed out. But the true treasures of love, relationships, faith, prayer, and devotion are a heritage that can be stored away. They will endure beyond this life.

Jesus said in Matthew 6:19-21: "Do not lay up for yourselves treasures on earth, where moth and rust destroy and where thieves break in and steal; but lay up for yourselves treasures in heaven, where neither moth nor rust destroys and where thieves do not break in and steal. For where your treasure is, there your heart will be also."

In other words, what really pays — in eternal dividends — is to remember and treasure the eternal truths from the Father's heavenly home.

Memo to myself:
— Polish the gilt-edged frame on the plaque in my bedroom

— Ask David to play the music to Mama's favorite hymn— while we both sing the words!
— Clean out the hall closet

Prayer:

Dear Jesus, thank You for the rich heritage You gave. May I never forget where real treasures can be found. Amen.

Before I forget—I'll do it today:

What treasures have you been given? To whom will you pass them?

What eternal truth have you been contemplating lately?

How can you begin to make this a legacy for someone today?

Chapter 15

Don't Forget to Serve!

"Serve the LORD with gladness. . . ."
(Ps. 100:2)

*Y*ou-nique. That's what you are.
God gave you an original, one-of-a-kind personality so that you could serve Him with gladness! Your style—your way of looking at things, your way of serving—is You-niquely you! Paul wrote: "There are diversities of gifts, but the same Spirit. There are differences of ministries, but the same Lord" (1 Cor. 12:4-5).

Each person is custom-crafted as a priceless work of art. The creativity that our Creator poured into us flows out in distinctive expressions.

When I announced that our next committee meeting would be at Joy's home, enthusiasm soared! Suddenly everyone would be able to come! Why was there such a spontaneous response?

Because we would get to see Joy's "natural habitat"—look at all her knickknacks, her color scheme, her country kitchen decor—we would get a firsthand opportunity to enjoy her own unique style. . . .

As the models swished onto the runway, out of courtesy I stifled a gasp. These clothes, at least so far, were simply not *my style*! Didn't they know about how a "Winter" had to resist every temptation to even consider purchasing a cream-colored jumpsuit?

As if the event sponsors could read my mind, out sauntered a high-style model in a royal blue tailored suit that captured my interest. It would suit the spring retreat schedule *stylishly*!

"Turn the mikes higher, Jan!" Barbara called to the back of the auditorium. The trio had taken a short break in their rehearsal for the evening program. Marge walked by and asked if I knew what the decibel level for safe hearing was. I didn't.

One of the greatest realities to my advancing age seems to be in my personal decibel level of appreciation of music. "To each her own" is a saying that is happily accommodated in lots of meetings as the *style* of music changes from guitars to organs — from folk to fanfare — majestic to mournful. *Vive la différence*!

The patients in the "unresponsive" ward at the rest home seemed to sense the difference when Millie arrived each Wednesday afternoon. She spread out the pretty flowered cloth, unwrapped her china teapot, and laid out the cookies. From bed to bed she served those listless people *with style*! Nothing on her schedule competed with this commitment — she simply arrived every week without fail.

It was puzzling to some of her friends. Millie seemed to actually glow with joy and anticipation as she shared the reflections of her time at the home, and how she needed to hurry to get ready to go again. Those involved in perhaps more visible ministries paused to thank God for Millie — and for her uniqueness.

Right now I'm looking at an old, eight-by-ten black and white photograph that is a precious reminder to me of the unique way God uses His people. In the portrait, the famous singer Kate Smith is beaming as she turns over a bundle of harmonicas to my mother-in-love. Dear Mother Hepburn in her Salvation Army bonnet and uniform and simple, wire-rimmed glasses is grinning with the joy that comes from a heart overflowing with glad service for her Lord.

On the table in front of these two servant women are boxes and bundles of harmonicas. Rose Hepburn was the wife of the divisional commander of the Salvation Army in Philadelphia. At the outset of World War II, when veterans began arriving at the newly established Valley Forge Hospital in Pennsylvania, Mother Hepburn began a program of visitation and encouragement to these veterans who were primarily blind.

Along with Mother, a group of Salvationists went every Monday evening, without fail, for twenty-six years until that hospital closed its doors. My husband remembers being sent as a young teen to entertain the hospitalized veterans with his trumpet.

On one of the visits Mother met a young man who had requested a harmonica. This was not unusual. Mother was teaching people how to restring violins and work with other musical instruments. Today it might be called "therapy," but then it was just Mother Hepburn's way of making those men feel confident and useful.

Well, Mother loved a challenge. She didn't know where to come up with harmonicas but was determined that God would provide. She prayed. Then God answered her prayer by giving her an idea. Somehow, in her own unique way, Mother got in touch with Kate Smith and asked if she could help.

On a radio station in Philadelphia, where Mother Hepburn hosted a broadcast called "The Home League of the Air," she made an appeal for harmonicas for the blinded veterans. With Kate Smith's celebrity status and the forum of the air waves, it was successful.

My husband says that as a young man, he was simply astounded. "I never saw anything like it. There were thousands of harmonicas. And so many different kinds! The response was so overwhelming that I wouldn't be surprised if everyone in Valley Forge had a harmonica in every pocket!"

Wouldn't you say that Mother Hepburn had a unique ministry? Over the years she took it upon herself to establish correspondence with those blinded veterans. Many recuperated and were sent to their home towns. When Mother would travel with Dad Hepburn in his ministry, she would often phone or even visit veterans in their homes.

When Mother went to heaven in 1974 we found a cross file, kept up-to-date, of over five thousand blinded veterans in our country she kept in touch with through at least a Christmas letter. Besides that, she managed to maintain a regular column in the *Blinded Veterans' Newspaper* entitled "Mrs. Hepburn Chats...." She always laughed about the time when, as a guest speaker, someone introduced her in all seriousness as "Mrs. Chats."

It was not surprising that Mother became Woman of the Year for the Veteran's Association in Washington. But her honors reflected treasures in heaven.

Only eternity will reveal the lives she influenced and encouraged through this rare ministry, which was certainly an adjunct to her full vocation as national director of women's ministries for the Salvation Army.

One Attitude; Many Modes

Mother Hepburn's example taught me that God has graciously gifted each of us with the ability of fulfilling His will individually in separate styles, but as character copies of the Lord Jesus Himself. We are instructed to have the attitude (which means mindset, perspective, behavior, and response) of Jesus Christ. God chooses to use our varieties of personalities, with all our quirks, to accomplish His purposes.

"There are many ways in which God works in our lives, but it is the same God who does the work in and through all of us who are his. The Holy Spirit displays God's power through each of us as a means of helping the entire church" (1 Cor. 12:6-7 TLB).

I consider it the World's Grandest Style Show — God's Spirit working through each of us as displays of His power to a waiting world. Put on the robe of His righteousness and the garments of praise. Consider Paul's challenge in 2 Timothy 4:2-6 to dress appropriately in the scriptural *style of a servant*:

- Preach the Word,
- being prepared in season and out of season,
- with great patience and careful instruction.
- Persevere — to perform all the duties of your ministry.

"For I am already being poured out as a drink offering. . . ."

Preach the Word

"Susie, how did you come to know Jesus? Whose preaching got the message through?"

"Nobody's *preaching*," Susie answered. "It was my Aunt Mary's *practicing* that showed me the Savior!"

Someone once said, "Preach the gospel — but use words only if you have to!" Getting the Word out is our number-one service as believers. But the only effective preaching is that which is effectively displayed in Spirit-controlled living. Our personal example is the loudest statement we make. Paul exhorted Timothy to respect the Word of God, allowing it to do its work shaping, styling, correcting, and equipping for good work.

Why do you think Paul could speak with such authority in his command to preach the Word? It is because he had earned the right as a model of the Word. As Paul faithfully looked to Christ as example, he established his credibility. He paid his dues; fought a good fight; finished his course; kept the faith.

What about us? Is my style like Paul's? Is your style of service commending the Word with credibility because you are modeling the message well? Consider the following Bible passage. Can you fill in these blank spaces in Ephesians 2:10 with your name?

_____ is God's [own] handiwork
(His workmanship), recreated in Christ Jesus, [born anew]
that _____ may do those good
works which God predestined (planned beforehand) for
_____, (taking paths which He pre-
pared ahead of time) that _____ should
walk in them."

(THE AMPLIFIED BIBLE)

Be Prepared in Season and out

Keep your sense of urgency (stand by, be at hand and
ready, whether the opportunity seems to be favorable or
unfavorable, whether it is convenient or inconvenient,
whether it be welcome or unwelcome, you as a preacher
of the Word are to show people in what way their lives are
wrong) and convince them, rebuking and correcting,
warning and urging and encouraging them, being unflagg-
ing and inexhaustible in patience and teaching.

(2 Tim. 4:2 THE AMPLIFIED BIBLE)

A tall order indeed! Paul challenges us to a deep personal
integrity and consistency of lifestyle. The preparation part, the
behind-the-scenes part, the investment of our time and energies,
requires a personal level of commitment rather uncommon these
days.

David and I were walking through the French Quarter of New
Orleans on a darkening, humid Sunday evening. Often when we
travel, we try to find a nearby church where we can worship. The

address was scribbled on a scrap of paper, and we kept checking it for directions through the unfamiliar streets. Then we saw it.

Jesus Saves.

A simple hand-painted sign was hanging outside the storefront chapel. It looked deserted so we peered through the small window on the front door, wondering if there was actually a service scheduled as the Yellow Pages had advertised. Rows of chairs were empty except for one man and woman kneeling in the front row. They got up as we entered.

"Welcome! Betty and I were just praying for some requests we received this week." He spoke as if to apologize for not being at the door. "We're so glad to have you. Where are you folks from?"

"We're just visiting New Orleans and looked in the phone book for a neighborhood church with a Sunday evening service. Will there be one?"

"Certainly! Betty and I were waiting to see if the Lord would bring anybody to us tonight. While we waited, we just prayed! But now, let's begin."

Without embarrassment or apology that dear pastor stepped to the podium and began the service. David and I sat in the front row. Betty played the piano and at the proper time her preacher husband delivered a well-prepared sermon in its entirety. We sang and sang, David played and sang, and I thanked the Lord for the clear witness and the sense of urgency — and dignity — and humility — and preparation displayed. God was truly honored.

Life is too short. Keep it simple. Get by. Don't work so hard. Wing it. Who really cares anyhow? The list is endless of those phrases that encourage *mediocrity* ... don't let them distract you from your pursuit of the *excellent*. Be prepared in season and out of season.

"Strength and honor are her clothing; / She shall rejoice in time to come" (Prov. 31:25).

Be Patient and Persevering

"For the time will come when they will not endure sound doctrine, but according to their own desires, because they have itching ears, they will heap up for themselves teachers" (2 Tim. 4:3).

Americans seem bent on worshiping at the shrine of self. "Have it your way!" "You owe it to yourself!" "You deserve a break today!" are just some of the advertising slogans that the media pump into our brains. With instant credit, we don't have to wait to satisfy our desires. "Get it now!"

Perhaps you've heard statistics like these: Americans spent more than forty billion dollars on personal care products last year. In contrast only twenty billion dollars was contributed to all of the nation's churches combined. The focus in our country is *self*. And people continue to feel unfulfilled.

Serving others is the only road to fulfillment in life. Sue prayed one lonely morning that God would let her be a help to someone. She was amazed that all day long people and prayer requests came to her door. A fourteen-year-old boy who had run away from home. A desperate friend whose marriage was falling apart. A senior citizen in need of care. That evening, Sue prayed another prayer:

> Lord, help me to retain
>   a memory
>   of this day,
>   so that on the "me" days
>   and the "I want" days,
>   and the "nobody notices me" days,
>   I will remember that
>   I like myself better on the
>   "let me be a help to others" days.
>   Amen.[1]

Serving with style means patiently persevering and letting go of selfish desires.

Performance Plus

Shirley lived on the outskirts of a little town in Oregon when she was a child. "Every Saturday, without fail, there came a knock on our door," she says. "Mr. Jones, the rural pastor for the American Sunday School Union Church, came by to invite our needy family to Sunday school.

"Mother never let us go — but Mr. Jones continued week after week, month after month, to stop by as if he had never been turned down before!"

Finally Shirley's mother relented. After all, if that man cared enough to come so many times, the only courteous thing to do was to visit the church — just once!

"Once was all we needed," Shirley told me. "The Lord got ahold of Mom and all of us!"

Knowing the Lord compels us to serve Him. We continue to perform in the face of opposition and discouragement. "The Lord grant mercy to the household of Onesiphorus, for he often refreshed me . . . he sought me out very zealously and found me. The Lord grant to him that he may find mercy from the Lord in that Day—and you know very well how many ways he ministered to me . . ." (2 Tim. 1:16-18).

It takes some doing to pursue opportunities to bring refreshment to someone in need. Often there will be more people clamoring for our attention than we have time or resources to accommodate. But persevering means faithfully performing your ministry—in Jesus' style.

Poured Out

> I'm a little teapot, short and stout
> Here is my handle; here is my spout.
> When I get all steamed up, then I shout:
> Just tip me over and pour me out!

That's the way the old song goes. For some reason one day I thought of those words when I was reading what Paul said, "I am already being poured out as a drink offering." I began to think of the vessel we must be if we are truly Christ's servants.

A china teapot or cup is inanimate. It is entirely under the control of its user. It doesn't pick itself up, fill itself, or pour itself out. The little teapot is readily available to the one who wants to use it. It doesn't resist.

That's how a servant should be. Ready. Useable.

Dear Lord Jesus,
I praise You for making me just as I am.
For putting me through the fire — again and again
until I find myself actually becoming
what You had in mind for me to be . . .
before the foundation of the earth.
Fill me once again — maintain control over
my life,
my thoughts,
my behavior,
my service . . .
Then use me — poured out — fulfilling Your
purposes, just as You promised.
                    Amen.

Memo to myself:

— Get out the old teapot and shine it up before our company comes tomorrow

—Look for David's harmonica and plan to visit the old folks' nursing home on Sunday. Maybe I can teach them to sing "Make Me a Servant"

Prayer:

Lord make me a servant . . . Amen.

Before I forget—I'll do it today:

What things do you do that could be called excellent?

What's one thing that you could change from mediocre to excellent, starting today?

*J*ust Wanted to Remind You . . .

"For this reason I will not be negligent to remind you always of these things. . . . Moreover, I will be careful to ensure that you always have a reminder of these things. . . ."
(2 Peter 1:12, 15)

"*W*hen are they coming? How much longer? Isn't it time yet?" A hurried and harried young mother finally clicked off the vacuum cleaner, stuffed the handle of her feather duster in her back jeans pocket, and responded to the impatient cries of her little girl.

"No, Honey," she comforted her anxious trooper, "Grandma and Grandpa said they'd be here at noon. That means when both hands of the clock are straight up—pointing to the number twelve—it'll be time to expect them. See? The little hand is only on number ten. That means we have two more hours. I know you're excited, Sweetie, but we just have to wait."

Four-year-old Lois had a thoughtful look on her face as she continued to gaze at the clock on the kitchen wall. Her mom smiled as she grabbed the vacuum handle, wondering if Lois would stare at that clock for the full two hours. How impatient children can be while mothers are thankful for every extra minute! There wasn't a corner of the house that didn't need some attention, and two more hours would lend just enough time to prepare lunch and make things presentable for company.

"Mom! It's time!" Lois was grabbing her mom's hand and tugging her toward the kitchen. It hadn't even been ten minutes, but sure enough, both hands on the bold-faced clock were pointing to the twelve. A stepping stool beneath the clock gave away Lois's secret. In her impatience she had climbed up and advanced the timepiece to suit her desires.

We Don't Know the Time

How hard it is to wait. Do you feel that too? We want time to go slowly when there is so much to be done. But oh how we want to speed it up when we are ready!

Jesus says in the book of Luke that it will be good for the servants when the Master returns and finds them ready. He reminds us that we need to keep our house in order—our spiritual house, above all. Peter reminded his readers that there was still time to wait but that with the Lord one day was like a thousand years and a thousand years like one day. God is not on our time schedule. And He reminded us to be ready at a moment's notice because Jesus is coming back.

We can't manipulate the hands on His eternal clock. Listen to what Peter said in his last letter to us:

> First, I want to remind you that in the last days there will
> come scoffers who will do every wrong they can think of,
> and laugh at the truth. This will be their line of argument:

"So Jesus promised to come back, did he? Then where is he? He'll never come! Why, as far back as anyone can remember everything has remained exactly as it was since the first day of creation."

They deliberately forget this fact: that God did destroy the world with a mighty flood, long after he had made the heavens by the word of his command, and had used the waters to form the earth and surround it. And God has commanded that the earth and the heavens be stored away for a great bonfire at the judgment day, when all ungodly men will perish....

The day of the Lord is surely coming, as unexpectedly as a thief, and then the heavens will pass away with a terrible noise and the heavenly bodies will disappear in fire, and the earth and everything on it will be burned up.

(2 Peter 3:3-7, 10 TLB)

An Important Question

Considering all of this, Peter poses a question that you and I should ask ourselves over and over. He says that since everything is going to be destroyed in this way, what kind of people ought we to be (v. 11)?

"You ought to live holy and godly lives as you look forward to the day of God and speed its coming. That day will bring about the destruction of the heavens by fire, and the elements will melt in the heat. But in keeping with his promise we are looking forward to a new heaven and a new earth, the home of righteousness" (2 Peter 3:11-13 NIV).

Peter was reminding his readers that we live on a different time warp than unbelievers. We know God will keep His promise. So, *what sort of people ought we to be?*

Let's get personal. What sort of woman ought I to be? What sort of woman ought you to be?

First—Be Holy

First, we ought to be holy. Set apart for Him. Clean, clear through. Pure in heart. Reflecting the very character of a holy God.

The words of an old hymn seem to be a workable outline for what sort of woman I ought to be in these days while waiting for His return.

> Take time to be holy, speak oft with thy Lord;
> Abide in Him always, and feed on His Word:
> Make friends of God's children; help those who are
>   weak;
> Forgetting in nothing His blessing to seek.
>
> Take time to be holy, the world rushes on;
> Spend much time in secret with Jesus alone.
> By looking to Jesus, like Him thou shalt be;
> Thy friends in thy conduct His likeness shall see.
>
> Take time to be holy, let Him be thy guide,
> And run not before Him, whatever betide.
> In joy or in sorrow, still follow thy Lord,
> And, looking to Jesus, still trust in His Word.[1]

Four Words

In my Bible there are four words over Colossians 3: *Rules for Holy Living.* As I think of this Scripture I often cannot help but remember the simplicity of these rules. When followed, they would certainly keep us ready for His coming:

- setting our hearts on what matters—on things above where our lives are already hidden with Christ in God;
- setting our minds on what matters—having allowed or kept our wills in submission to His and allowing our minds to be constantly in transformation and renewal (see Rom. 12:2);
- putting to death whatever belongs to our earthly nature;
- clothing ourselves with kindness, compassion, humility, and patience because we are God's holy and loved people;
- letting the peace of God rule in our hearts;
- letting the Word of God dwell inside of us—richly!
- doing whatever we do in the name of the Lord Jesus.

Junk the Grave Clothes

I've written in the margin of my Bible, "Put off the grave clothes and put on the grace clothes." When I look at this list of rules for living a holy life, a very practical suggestion comes to mind: Take some three-by-five cards and write on them in large, bold letters one of these characteristics of the holy life, compassion or kindness, and then perhaps include a verse of Scripture that relates to that character quality.

Can't you imagine hanging one on your refrigerator door or your dashboard in the car and working on one of these qualities in everyday life? Bringing it into focus. Setting your mind on it. I might do one character quality a month until it becomes a part of the dailiness of my life.

One of the character qualities that the Word of God reminds me to implement is patience. Romans 5 tells us that patience develops through suffering. As patience completes its work, it produces the character of God.

It's easy to see that most of the time the way God produces His character traits in us is by giving us opportunities to develop them. It would be so much easier if He would simply zap us and declare us holy! Instead, as we dress in the righteousness of Jesus Christ and allow His character to be formed in us, we have increasing awareness of His power as these special qualities develop.

Mobile Homes for God

What sort of woman ought I to be? One who is living a godly life. C.S. Lewis wrote:

> I think that many of us, when Christ has enabled us to overcome one or two sins that were an obvious nuisance, are inclined to feel (though we do not put it into words) that we are now good enough. He has done all we wanted him to do, and we should be obliged if he would now leave us alone.
>
> But the question is not what we intended ourselves to be, but what he intended us to be when he made us . . .
>
> Imagine yourself as a living house. God comes in to

rebuild that house. At first, perhaps, you can understand what he is doing. He is getting the drains right and stopping the leaks in the roof and so on: you knew that those jobs needed doing and so you are not surprised. But presently he starts knocking the house about in a way that hurts abominably and does not seem to make sense. What on earth is he up to? The explanation is that he is building quite a different house from the one you thought of— throwing out a new wing here, putting on an extra floor there, running up towers, making courtyards. You thought you were going to be made into a decent little cottage; but he is building a palace. He intends to come and live in it himself.[2]

I must be a woman in whom the presence of God dwells. How mind-boggling to think God would allow me to be a "mobile home" for His presence! That's what *holy* means—a dwelling place for God. Set apart for the highest and holiest of privileges. Second Corinthians 2 records these lovely words:

> But thanks be to God! For through what Christ has done, he has triumphed over us so that now wherever we go he uses us to tell others about the Lord and to spread the Gospel like a sweet perfume. As far as God is concerned there is a sweet, wholesome fragrance in our lives. It is the fragrance of Christ within us, an aroma to both the saved and the unsaved all around us.
>
> (2 Cor. 2:14-15 TLB)

A Sweet Fragrance

As we move about through our world we have the benefit,

without self-effort, of being the fragrant awareness of Jesus Christ.

Karen and I were staying in a posh Las Vegas hotel. (It's not what you think!) We were speaking at a conference and were accommodated in a fancy hotel which had a good share of its first floor devoted to casinos.

We steered clear as we found our way to the breakfast cafe. Just before we indulged in our English muffins and coffee we bowed our heads and thanked God for the food as well as the challenging day that was before us. After breakfast, as we were walking past the section of phone booths and the omnipresent slot machines, a lady approached us. She was wearing lovely jewelry and an orchid-colored turban hat and I thought, "My, she must be well off."

Though we did not know her, it was evident that she had been waiting for us. We were expecting to meet our host at the curb, and as this woman approached I supposed she was going to tell me I had dropped something. I didn't at all anticipate her pointed question.

"Were you the women who prayed in the cafe?" she inquired.

"Yes," I smiled, "we certainly did."

"Whom did you pray to?"

"Well, I prayed to the Lord Jesus and to our dear heavenly Father."

"Oh," she paused, looking like she still wanted to converse, but couldn't seem to form the words. Underneath the lovely hat her face seemed lined with worry and concern. She was slow to offer any other questions so I asked her, "Do you know Jesus?"

"Well, I know he was a Jew, and I know a little bit about Jews because I lived in Israel for a while."

"Did anyone ever tell you that you can know Him personally?" I asked.

Our conversation went back and forth for a few minutes as I tried to draw her out, sensing that since she had waited specifically for us to leave the cafe there must have been something special that she wanted. She told me her name was Monica.

"Monica, is there something you need to have the Lord do for you? Do you have a special concern?"

"Well, my daughter is in terrible trouble in Los Angeles. I'm so mad at her that I just want to kill her, and I don't know what to do."

I listened a little longer. She so obviously needed to share her heavy burden. Before we parted I reached into my purse for a tract I had with me called "Facing Life's Fears." Then I asked if I could pray for her and for her daughter. I explained the simple principles of how she could know Jesus personally. We prayed together.

As Karen and I moved through our day, Monica came to my mind often. I prayed that God would make Himself very real to Monica and that she would soon come to a sweet, saving knowledge of His presence in her life. What a simple thing we had done to identify ourselves — just bowing our heads and praying over English muffins.

Secondly—Be Grace-full!

You and I ought to be women who are growing in grace and in our knowledge of the Lord Jesus Christ. The apostle Peter lists a ladder of characteristics that will cause us to be ready for Jesus' imminent coming. Climbing these steps will lead to grace and the full knowledge of Jesus Christ:

Step 1: Add to your faith goodness, so you can "know God better and discover what he wants you to do."

Step 2: "Learn to put aside your own desires so that you will become patient and godly, gladly letting God have his way with you."

Step 3: The next step is for you to "enjoy other people and to like them," and finally to love them as God does.

Step 4: Keep going in this way so that you can become "strong spiritually and become fruitful and useful to our Lord Jesus Christ" (2 Peter 1:5-8 TLB).

What sort of women ought we to be? Holy women. Grace-filled women. Annie Johnson Flint wrote the beautiful hymn, "He Giveth More Grace":

> He giveth more grace when the burdens grow greater;
> He sendeth more strength when the labors increase.
> To added affliction He addeth His Mercy
> To multiplied trials, His multiplied peace.
>
> His Love has no limit; His grace has no measure;
> His power has no boundary known unto men.
> For out of His infinite riches in Jesus,
> He giveth, and giveth, and giveth again.[3]

Last of All—Be Ready

What sort of woman ought I to be? Until He comes — a woman who is ready. What an urgent time we live in. Never was it more apparent to me than on January 16 of last year. Four friends and I were planning to meet at the San Francisco airport to begin a journey to England. Many months previously I had made a commitment to fly to Lakenheath Air Force Base to minister at a retreat for women of the AFB chapels in England.

As David was tossing my luggage into the trunk of our car, our neighbors drove up to say that the first bombs had been dropped in Iraq. What a sense of urgency we felt as we wondered whether or not it was even safe to go.

When we touched down on British soil, the awareness of war was in the air and all around. Tanks at the airport curb with soldiers alerted to the possibility of terrorism were grim reminders we were in a world at war. Later we met in our own special Upper Room at the base chapel. Most of the women there had husbands already deployed to Saudi Arabia.

There was, in fact, a sense of urgency about all we were doing. What sort of women ought we to be? Because of the gravity of the hour — ready. Ready for anything. Philippians 4:13 in the Phillips translation says, "I am ready for anything because of the spirit of the one who lives within me."

Ready for anything. R-F-A. How, I wondered as I looked into the faces of those concerned wives and wondered what I could say to comfort them, how do you get ready for anything?

1.   By practicing the presence of God. We've talked about it

already. Learning to live in His presence every minute. Paul said, "Pray without ceasing" (1 Thess. 5:17). Oswald Chambers adds, "If we think of prayer as the breath in our lungs and the blood from our hearts, we think rightly."[4]

2. By feeding on His promises. I have Scripture memory cassette tapes on topics such as controlling the tongue, prayer, using time wisely, and worry-free living. They have been a source of encouragement to me. Memorizing Scripture is a way of reprogramming the mind for strength and stability in these difficult times. Appropriating His Word, knowing it, learning it, and practicing it will keep us R.F.A.!

3. By having a partnership with believers. We need each other. Ray Ortlund wrote, "The greatest resource that you and I have is the presence of Jesus Christ Himself. The second most precious possession is the fellowship of God's people."[5]

How we realized that truth as we met together and prayed and looked into the Word of God and then created a support system. We didn't know what tomorrow would hold for those dear women. We wanted to be R.F.A.

And when we remembered the Scripture says we belong to each other and each needs all of the others, we became more aware that perhaps husbands would not come back — or at least not the same men that they had left. They needed to be keeping short accounts, encouraging one another as they faced the variety of possibilities ahead of them.

What sort of women ought we to be? Women who are expecting the Lord's return at any moment and are ready. I have a little sign that was given to me so I could hang it on my front door should the need arise. On one side it says "Will return" and then there is a clock with hands on it that you can move about to show visitors when you will be back. You've seen them.

Well, I thought about using it, but instead it has become a reminder to me of the promise of God. What I have done is simply remove both hands from the face of that clock. The sign still promises "Will return." The hour is not certain.

The promise is there, friend. Jesus will return. My part and yours is to be ready. For we don't know the day or the hour, but He reminds us over and over that times are urgent.

The name on an antique shop I have visited is: *Remains To Be Seen*. What a reminder to me. The Lord is coming! I don't know when. I don't understand exactly how. But what I shall become when I see Him face to face . . . remains to be seen!

In the lovely Phillips translation, Romans 8:18 says, "The whole creation is on tiptoe to see the wonderful sights of the sons of God coming into their own." Our natural tendency is to want to move the hands on the clock ourselves to make the time go faster. Instead, let us simply live on tiptoe with the expectation that He is coming soon. Live expectantly. Remember the Lord. Count on His promises. Don't forget to praise Him.

Don't forget all His benefits.

I know you knew all these things!

I just wanted to remind you . . .

before I forget. . . .

Memo to myself:

— *Review this week's schedule*

—*Read again 1 and 2 Thessalonians to refresh my memory!*

—*Spread some potpourri around the house as a reminder*

Prayer:
 Lord, help me to plan as if I have years ahead but live as if You were coming today. Help me get ready . . . in the twinkling of an eye. . . . Amen.

Before I forget—I'll do it today:
 In what ways is God making you a palace? How can you submit to this today?
 What's keeping you from being ready for anything? How can you prepare yourself today?

Notes

Chapter Two: Done . . . What?
1. John Newton, "Amazing Grace," public domain.
2. Reverend E. A. Hoffman, "Glory to His Name," public domain.
3. Lewis Smedes, *How Can It Be All Right When Everything's Wrong?* (San Francisco: Harper & Row, 1982), 3.
4. Peter Gilquist, *Love Is Now* (Grand Rapids: Zondervan, 1970).

Chapter Three: He Remembers to Heal
1. "Because He Lives." Words by William J. and Gloria Gaither. Music by William J. Gaither. © Copyright 1971 by William J. Gaither. All rights reserved. Used by permission.
2. Charles H. Gabriel, "O That Will Be Glory," public domain.
3. *The 700 Club*, February 20, 1990.
4. A. B. Simpson, "Himself," from *Hymns of the Christian Life* (Camp Hill, Penn.: Christian Publications, 1977). Used by permission.

Chapter Four: Satisfaction Guaranteed
1. Annie Chapman, "Five Ways to Eliminate Envy," *Today's Christian Woman*, September/October 1991, 69. Used by permission.

Chapter Six: The Love Gift
1. Ruth Harms Calkin, prayer from back cover of *Lord, You Love to Say Yes* (Wheaton: Tyndale House Publishers, 1976).
2. E. Stanley Jones, *The Divine Yes* (Nashville: Abingdon Press, 1975), 22.

Chapter Seven: Forget Past Achievements, Failures, and You-Know-Who
1. Karen Burton Mains, used by permission.
2. Sally Chesham, used by permission.

Chapter Eight: Remember: Marshmallows First
  1. Evelyn Minshull, author of novels for children, church programs, and adult biblical novels. Used by permission.
  2. Isobel Kuhn, poem from the book By Searching (Littleton, Colo.: OMF Books, 1959), 5. Used by permission.

Chapter Nine: A Wreath on the Chimney
  1. Duane L. Storey, "Celebrate Your Memories," *Virtue* magazine, January/February 1990.

Chapter Eleven: Remember the Children!
  1. *The Elisabeth Elliot Newsletter* (Ann Arbor: Servant Publications) November/December 1991. Used by permission.
  2. Ibid.
  3. Nancy Gibbs, "Do We Care About Our Kids?" *Time*, October 8, 1990.
  4. Ibid.
  5. Ibid.
  6. From *Amy Carmichael of Dohnavur* by Amy Carmichael. Published by Christian Literature Crusade, used by permission.

Chapter Twelve: Take Out the Garbage
  1. Author unknown, from The Barbara Johnson's *Love-lines* newsletter/Spatula Ministries, Box 444, La Habra, CA 90631.
  2. Mark Pantinkin, "House blindness: If it's been there long enough, it isn't there," *Providence Journal*.
  3. James W. Skillen, "The Agony in the City," *Moody Monthly*, January 1990, 24.
  4. Ibid.
  5. Joseph Stowell, "Thinking Right in a World Gone Wrong," *Moody Monthly*, January 1990, 4.

Chapter Thirteen: Don't Forget to Pray
  1. Lois Johnson, *Either Way I Win* (Minneapolis: Augsburg Publishing House, 1979), page 32.

2. Brother Lawrence, *The Practice of the Presence of God* (Old Tappan: Spire Books, 1979), 8.
3. Major Della Rees, "Calling All Prayer Warriors?" *New Frontier*, Salvation Army newsletter.
4. Ibid.

Chapter Fourteen: Remember What You Learned At Home
1. *Love-lines*, Barbara Johnson's newsletter/Spatula Ministries, Box 444, La Habra, CA 90631. Used by permission.
2. Buryl Red & Grace Hawthorne, "It's Cool in the Furnace," © Copyright 1973 by Word Music (a division of WORD, INC.). All rights reserved. Used by permission.

Chapter Fifteen: Don't Forget to Serve
1. Sue G. Laramore, *Decision* magazine, November 1990. Used by permission.

Finally: "Just Wanted to Remind You ..."
1. William D. Longstaff, "Take Time to Be Holy," public domain.
2. C.S. Lewis, *Mere Christianity* (New York: Macmillan, 1978; London: Collins Fount, Harper Collins Publishers Limited, 1978).
3. "He Giveth More Grace" by Hubert C. Mitchell, Annie Johnson Flint © 1941. Renewed 1969, Lillenas Publishing Company/SESAC. All rights reserved. Used by permission of Integrated Copyright Group, Inc.
4. Oswald Chambers, *My Utmost for His Highest* (New York: Dodd Mead, 1935), 147.
5. Ray Ortlund, *Make My Life a Miracle* (Glendale: Regal Books, 1974), 60.

About the Authors

Daisy Hepburn is a writer and speaker who shares motivating and encouraging ideas with women across the country. Her dynamic style is known to captivate audiences at a variety of conventions and retreats throughout the year.

The author of *What's So Glorious About Everyday Living?*, *How to Grow a Women's Minis-tree*, and the *Life With Spice Bible Study Series*, Daisy and her husband David live in San Francisco, California.

Lou Ann Smith is a graduate of the Christian Writer's Guild in Hume, California and has been published in periodicals such as *Decision*, *Moody Monthly*, and *Christian Parenting Today*. Besides traveling as a speaker for Christian Women's Clubs and church retreats, Lou Ann is a wife, homemaker, Bible study teacher, and mother of two teenagers.